Programming Fundamentals Using Microsoft® Visual Basic .NET

Gary B. Shelly
Thomas J. Cashman
Jeffrey J. Quasney

THOMSON
COURSE TECHNOLOGY

COURSE TECHNOLOGY
25 THOMSON PLACE
BOSTON MA 02210

SHELLY
CASHMAN
SERIES®

Australia • Canada • Denmark • Japan • Mexico • New Zealand • Philippines • Puerto Rico • Singapore
South Africa • Spain • United Kingdom • United States

THOMSON

COURSE TECHNOLOGY

Programming Fundamentals
Using Microsoft® Visual Basic .NET
Gary B. Shelly
Thomas J. Cashman
Jeffrey J. Quasney

Executive Director:
Cheryl Costantini

Senior Acquisitions Editor:
Dana Merk

Senior Editor:
Alexandra Arnold

Product Manager:
David Rivera

Editorial Assistant:
Selena Coppock

Senior Manufactuing Coordinator :
Laura Burns

Series Consulting Editor:
Jim Quasney

Senior Production Editor:
Aimee Poirier

Development Editor:
Lisa Strite

Copy Editor:
Lyn Markowicz

Proofreader:
Nancy Lamm

Cover Image:
John Still

Compositor:
GEX Publishing Services

Indexer:
Cristina Haley

Programming Fundamentals Using Microsoft® Visual Basic .NET

Contents

APPENDIX A

Flowcharting and Pseudocode

APPENDIX B

Exploring the Visual Basic .NET IDE and Debugging

APPENDIX C

General Forms of Common Visual Basic .NET Statements, Data Types, and Naming Conventions

APPENDIX D

Programming Fundamentals Best Practices

Preface

The Shelly Cashman Series® offers the finest textbooks in computer education. We are proud of the fact that our previous programming textbooks have been so well received by computer educators. With each new programming text, we have made significant improvements based on the programming language enhancements and comments made by instructors and students. This text continues with the innovation, quality, and reliability that you have come to expect from the Shelly Cashman Series.

In this programming fundamentals book, you will find an educationally sound, highly visual, and easy-to-follow pedagogy that allows the student to begin designing and writing programs almost immediately. Heavy emphasis is placed on producing well-written and readable programs. A disciplined coding style is used consistently in all sample programs. Each chapter begins by presenting a problem, followed by a design of the solution and corresponding program solution. The remainder of the chapter discusses the program solution in small sections of code so that the student does not get lost in a maze of code. This discussion is accompanied by additional examples of programming techniques and *Best Practices* recommendations. The end-of-chapter material contains a wealth of short answer, online, and programming exercises to ensure your students have all the reinforcement they need.

Objectives of This Textbook

Programming Fundamentals Using Microsoft Visual Basic .NET is intended for use in combination with other books in a *Computer Concepts* course or *Programming Logic* course or in a one-credit hour *Introduction to Programming* course. No mathematics beyond the high school level is required. This book was written for the student with average ability, for which continuity, simplicity, and practicality were considered essential. Specific objectives of this book are as follows:

- To teach students how to design and implement program solutions using Microsoft Visual Basic .NET
- To acquaint the student with good problem-solving techniques that can be used with any programming language
- To use practical problems to illustrate how to design and implement program solutions
- To emphasize the basic logic constructs that serve as models for future program development
- To encourage independent study and help those who are working alone in a distance education environment

The Shelly Cashman Approach

Features of the Shelly Cashman Series *Programming Fundamentals Using Microsoft Visual Basic .NET* book include:

- **Unique Pedagogy:** This book employs a unique pedagogy, whereby each chapter presents a complete sample program, which is then broken down into pieces and discussed in detail over the remainder of the chapter. Each sample program is preceded by a flowchart or pseudocode. The presentation of each of the Visual Basic .NET statements required to complete a task in the sample program includes an easy-to-understand table with a general form and examples of its use.

- **Emphasis on Programming Fundamentals:** Through the use of examples, this book emphasizes such introductory programming topics as constructing readable programs, variable name selection, expression evaluation, implementation of the If...Then...Else construct, implementation of the Do While and Do Until constructs, and creation of simple application interfaces.

- **Thoroughly Tested Projects:** Unparalleled quality is assured because every figure in the book is produced by the author, and then each project must pass Course Technology's award-winning Quality Assurance program.

- **Best Practices:** More than 30 boxed tips found throughout the book and summarized in Appendix D highlight the recommended ways to code programs in Visual Basic .NET.

- **Integration of the World Wide Web:** The Learn It Online section at the end of each chapter integrates the World Wide Web into the student's learning experience. The Learn It Online section includes reinforcement exercises, learning games, and other types of online student activities.

Organization of This Textbook

Programming Fundamentals Using Microsoft Visual Basic .NET provides detailed instruction on how to design and implement a solution using Visual Basic .NET. The material is divided into four chapters and four appendices as follows:

Chapter 1 – An Introduction to Programming   Chapter 1 introduces students to a simple program. The chapter begins with the proper design of a Commission Calculator Console application and teaches students how to create a new Console application project in the Visual Basic .NET environment. Topics include program development methodology; working in the Visual Basic .NET programming environment; starting a new project; writing code; comment statements; variables and data types; Console application input and output; assignment statements; numeric expressions and operator precedence; and saving, testing, and printing a program.

Chapter 2 – Decision Making   Chapter 2 presents an overview of the fundamental concept involved with decision making in programming, including If...Then...Else and Select Case structures. The chapter also introduces constants. The Commission Calculator program is updated to make a decision on the commission rate depending on certain conditions. Topics include coding an If...Then...Else statement; coding a Select Case statement; declaring and using constants; using relational operators in code; and using logical operators in code.

Chapter 3 – Repetition and Arrays   Chapter 3 introduces students to the fundamental programming concepts involved with repetition structures, including Do While, Do Until, and For...Next loops. The chapter also introduces one-dimensional and multidimensional arrays. The Commission Calculator program is enhanced to process multiple records from an array, print a report to a Console window, and provide totals. Topics include coding a Do Until loop; coding a Do While loop; coding a For...Next loop; using one-dimensional and multidimensional arrays; and coding arithmetic concatenation operators.

Chapter 4 – Windows Applications and Function Procedures   Chapter 4 provides an overview of Windows application development using Visual Basic .NET. The Commission Calculator program is made into a Windows application that uses four different types of controls. Topics include creating a new Windows application; changing form properties; adding controls to a form; moving, resizing, and deleting controls; changing properties of controls; writing code for an event procedure; calling a function procedure with parameters; and coding a new function procedure.

Appendices This book concludes with four appendices. Appendix A covers program design tools, including flowcharting and pseudocode. Appendix B introduces students to the Visual Basic .NET integrated development environment, including setting proper screen resolution and debugging. Appendix C summarizes the Visual Basic .NET statements introduced in the book and naming conventions for data types and controls. Appendix D summarizes the Best Practices tips that are introduced throughout the book.

End-of-Project Student Activities

A notable strength of the Shelly Cashman Series programming books is the extensive student activities at the end of each project. Well-structured student activities can make the difference between students merely participating in a class and students retaining the information they learn. The following activities are included in this book.

- **Chapter Summary** This section summarizes what was learned in the chapter. It provides a perfect first step chapter review for students.

- **Key Terms** The technologies and terms summarized in this section are those that students will encounter directly or indirectly on examinations.

- **Homework Assignments** The homework assignments are divided into two sections: *Short Answer* and *Learn It Online*. The *Short Answer* section includes determining numeric values, expression evaluation, valid variable selection, valid statement selection, reading partial flowcharts, and much more. The *Learn It Online* section consists of seven exercises. These exercises utilize the Web to offer project-related reinforcement activities that will help students gain confidence in their programming abilities. They include True/False, Multiple Choice, Short Answer, Practice Test, Learning Games, Newsgroup usage, Expanding Your Horizons, and Search Sleuth.

- **Programming Assignments** Several programming assignments per chapter require students to apply the knowledge gained in the chapter.

Instuctor Resources

The Shelly Cashman Series is dedicated to providing you with all of the tools you need to make your class a success. Information on all supplementary materials is available through your Course Technology representative or by calling one of the following telephone numbers: Colleges and Universities, 1-800-648-7450; High Schools, 1-800-824-5179; Private Career Colleges, 1-800-347-7707; Canada, 1-800-268-2222; Corporations with IT Training Centers, 1-800-648-7450; and Government Agencies, Health-Care Organizations, and Correctional Facilities, 1-800-477-3692.

Instructor Resources CD-ROM

The Instructor Resources for this textbook include both teaching and testing aids. The contents of each item on the Instructor Resources CD-ROM (ISBN 0-619-25515-3) are described below.

- **Instructor's Manual** The Instructor's Manual is made up of Microsoft Word files, which include detailed lesson plans with page number references, lecture notes, teaching tips, classroom activities, discussion topics, projects to assign, and transparency references. The transparencies are available through the Figure Files described on the next page.

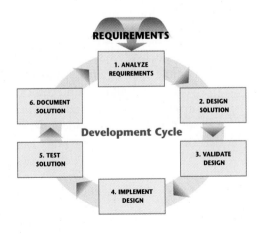

- **Syllabus**   Sample syllabi, which can be customized easily to a course, are included. The syllabi cover policies, class and lab assignments and exams, and procedural information.

- **Figure Files**   Illustrations for every figure in the textbook are available in electronic form. Use this ancillary to present a slide show in lecture or to print transparencies for use in lecture with an overhead projector. If you have a personal computer and LCD device, this ancillary can be an effective tool for presenting lectures.

- **PowerPoint Presentations**   PowerPoint Presentations is a multimedia lecture presentation system that provides PowerPoint slides for each project. Presentations are based on project objectives. Use this presentation system to present well-organized lectures that are both interesting and knowledge based. PowerPoint Presentations provides consistent coverage at schools that use multiple lecturers.

- **Solutions to Exercises**   Solutions are included for the end-of-project exercises, as well as the Project Reinforcement exercises.

- **Test Bank & Test Engine**   The ExamView test bank includes 110 questions for every project (25 multiple choice, 50 true/false, and 35 completion) with page number references, and when appropriate, figure references. A version of the test bank you can print also is included. The test bank comes with a copy of the test engine, ExamView, the ultimate tool for your objective-based testing needs. ExamView is a state-of-the-art test builder that is easy to use. ExamView enables you to create paper-, LAN-, or Web-based tests from test banks designed specifically for your Course Technology textbook. Utilize the ultra-efficient QuickTest Wizard to create tests in less than five minutes by taking advantage of Course Technology's question banks, or customize your own exams from scratch.

- **Additional Activities for Students**   These additional activities consist of Project Reinforcement Exercises, which are true/false, multiple choice, and short answer questions that help students gain confidence in the material learned.

Online Content

Course Technology offers textbook-based content for Blackboard, WebCT, and MyCourse 2.1

- **Blackboard and WebCT**   As the leading provider of IT content for the Blackboard and WebCT platforms, Course Technology delivers rich content that enhances your textbook to give your students a unique learning experience. Course Technology has partnered with WebCT and Blackboard to deliver our market-leading content through these state-of-the-art online learning platforms. Course Technology offers customizable content in every subject area, from computer concepts to PC repair.

- **MyCourse 2.1**   MyCourse 2.1 is Course Technology's powerful online course management and content delivery system. Completely maintained and hosted by Thomson, MyCourse 2.1 delivers an online learning environment that is completely secure and provides superior performance. MyCourse 2.1 allows nontechnical users to create, customize, and deliver World Wide Web-based courses; post content and assignments; manage student enrollment; administer exams; track results in the online gradebook; and more. With MyCourse 2.1, you easily can create a customized course that will enhance every learning experience.

An Introduction to Programming

Objectives

You will have mastered the material in this chapter when you can:

- Describe program development and identify the phases in the development cycle
- Define an algorithm
- Start Visual Basic .NET, describe the Visual Basic .NET IDE, and create a new program
- Describe Visual Basic .NET data types and declare variables within code

- Use arithmetic expressions that follow the order of operator precedence
- Write code to display prompts, accept input, and display output in the Console window
- Save, test, and document a program
- Use Visual Basic .NET Help

Introduction

Before a computer can produce a desired result, it must have a step-by-step series of instructions that tells it exactly what to do. The step-by-step series of instructions is called a **program**. A program accepts input, performs processing, and then produces output. The process of writing the sets of instructions for the computer to follow is called **programming**. A **programmer**, also called a **software developer**, designs and writes programs. An **application** (also called a software application) is a collection of one or more programs that is designed to complete a specific task, such as word processing or accounting. The term, application, also is used to refer to the version of a program that is distributed or sold to users. The process of using a programming language or programming environment to build software applications is called **program development**.

Microsoft Visual Basic .NET encompasses a set of tools and technologies that help developers build programs quickly. Visual Basic .NET's user-friendly programming environment, along with the relative simplicity of its programming language, allows individuals with little programming experience to create a wide range of programs.

After completing this chapter, you should be able to start Visual Basic .NET, describe the components of the Visual Basic .NET environment, and run a program from within the Visual Basic .NET environment. You also will learn how to start and describe the components of a Visual Basic .NET **project**, which is a collection of code and other files that usually encompasses one program. The chapter will cover how to design and then implement a program that interacts with the user. In writing the program, you will understand how to write Visual Basic .NET code and document the code with comment statements. You also will learn about the different data types used in Visual Basic .NET and how to write code that performs mathematical operations. You also will learn how to save, run, test, and document the program. Finally, you will learn how to use Visual Basic .NET Help.

An Overview of Programming

Programmers do not sit down and start writing code as soon as they have a programming assignment. Instead, they follow a series of steps, or phases, collectively referred to as the **development cycle**. The development cycle follows an organized plan, or **methodology**, that breaks the development cycle into a series of tasks. Many formal program development methodologies are available to programmers.

The methodology used in this book breaks the development cycle into six phases as shown in Table 1-1. When the testing phase identifies errors or new requirements are demanded of the program, a new iteration of the cycle begins with analyzing the requirements. In the discussion that follows, the term, program, is used to describe the result of the development cycle. An application, which is made up of one or more programs, also can be the result of the development cycle.

Table 1-1 The Development Cycle

PHASE		DESCRIPTION
1	Analyze requirements	Verify that the requirements are complete and translate user requirements into technical requirements, including descriptions of the program's inputs, processing, outputs, and interface.
2	Design solution	Develop a detailed, logical plan using a tool such as a flowchart or pseudocode. Design the user interface for the application, including input areas, output areas, and other necessary elements.
3	Validate design	Step through the solution design with test data. Receive confirmation from the user that the design solves the problem in a satisfactory manner.
4	Implement design	Translate the design into a program using a programming language or programming environment; include internal documentation, or comments, which are notes within the code that explain the purpose of code statements.
5	Test solution	Test the program, finding and correcting errors (also called **debugging**) until it is error free and contains enough safeguards to ensure the desired results.
6	Document solution	Review and, if necessary, revise internal documentation. Formalize and complete end-user (external) documentation.

Program requirements drive the development cycle. Requirements are supplied by the program's users or a representative of the users and are presented in a requirements document that describes how a particular problem can be solved by a program. A **requirements document** lists the functions and features that the program must provide for its users. Requirements include a statement of purpose for the requested program (also called a problem definition), the equations the program must use, and an explanation of how the program should respond to user interaction.

Designing the Commission Calculator Program

As you have learned, a program accepts input, performs processing, and then produces output. This chapter describes the development cycle for a program that calculates the sales commission due to a salesperson based on a commission rate, the total amount of sales, and the total value of the items returned by customers. The inputs for the program are the total sales and the total value of the items returned. The processing involves the calculation of the commission. The output includes the commission due to the salesperson.

Figure 1-1 shows the flowchart for the Commission Calculator program, and Figure 1-2 shows the corresponding Visual Basic .NET code for the program. Figure 1-3a shows the input prompts and input for the Commission

Calculator program. When you **run**, or **execute**, a program, the program is loaded into memory and the program code is executed. The program runs in a **Console window**, which has a text-based interface that allows users to enter input using the keyboard and displays output as text. A prompt in the first line of the Console window requests that the user enter the total sales in dollars. The user enters the total sales and then presses the ENTER key. A second prompt then requests that the user enter the total returns in dollars.

After the user enters the second input data item and then presses the ENTER key, the program performs the processing to calculate the commission. For the Commission Calculator program, the commission is equal to 14% of the total sales minus the total returns, and the calculation is expressed by the following equation:

Commission = .14 × (Total Sales – Total Returns)

Figure 1-3b shows the output produced by the program after it performs the calculation based on the input values shown in Figure 1-3a. The program writes a line indicating that the calculated commission is 1610 (that is, $1,610), followed by a line prompting the user to press a key to continue. The program then pauses until the user presses a key. After the user presses a key, the program halts execution and the Console window closes automatically.

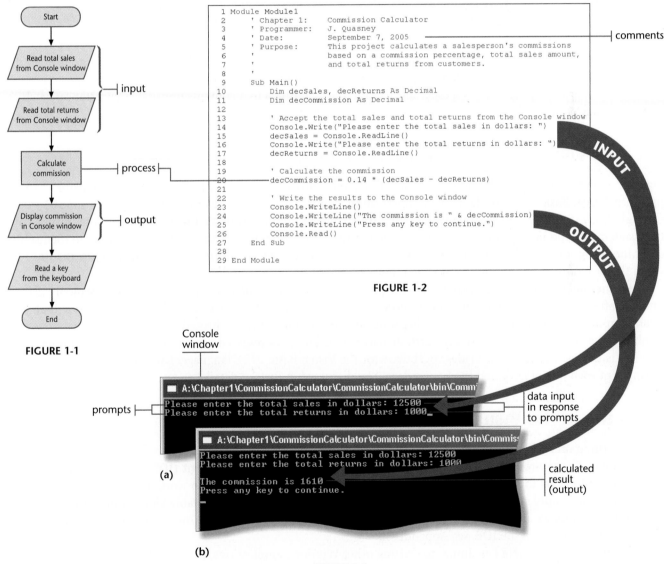

FIGURE 1-1

FIGURE 1-2

(a)

(b)

FIGURE 1-3

Flowcharts

Programmers often create a diagram or picture called a **flowchart** that graphically represents the logic used to develop an algorithm. An **algorithm** is the method or solution chosen to solve a problem. As shown in Figure 1-1 on the previous page, a flowchart consists of a standard set of symbols used to represent various steps or operations in a program's logic. When you draw a complete flowchart, you must begin with a terminal symbol that is then connected by a flowline to the first logical step in the problem solution. Most of the time, each step required to solve a problem is represented by a separate symbol. Appendix A includes a more detailed discussion of how to develop flowcharts.

Figure 1-1 shows the flowchart for the Commission Calculator program. After the terminal symbol indicating the start of the program, the first two operations are to read the two input items from the Console window. Next, the commission is calculated. The program then displays the results and pauses until the user presses a key on the keyboard.

> **Best Practices**
>
> Use flowcharts or pseudocode to solidify the design of every program you develop. Continue to use and update the flowcharts or pseudocode as you enhance or modify the program.

The third step of the development cycle is to validate the design. One way to validate the design is to use sample input data to step through the flowchart or pseudocode. You should validate the design of a program by using as many test scenarios as possible, being especially careful to use test data that contains unusual circumstances, such as very high data values, very low data values, negative values, or zero.

An Overview of a Visual Basic .NET Program

Figure 1-2 on the previous page shows the Visual Basic .NET program code for the Commission Calculator program. Visual Basic .NET displays line numbers on the left of the code to assist in reading the code. Lines 2 through 8, 13, 19, and 22 are comments. A **comment** is a note within the code that helps to explain the purpose of code statements and helps to document the meaning of the code. Programmers use comments as notes to themselves and other programmers about the meaning of the code. Any code used for comments does not execute; that is, when the program is run, the comment code is ignored.

All other lines of code are executed when the program is run. The code in the program executes sequentially, one line after the next, from the top to the bottom. As shown in Figure 1-2, the code includes lines of code that handle input (lines 14 through 17), processing (line 20), and output (lines 23 through 25). The words that appear in blue in the code are keywords. A **keyword**, such as Sub or Dim, is a reserved word that has special meaning within Visual Basic .NET and provides vocabulary for the Visual Basic .NET language. Later in this chapter, the meaning of each line of code and the keywords will be discussed in further detail.

Working in the Visual Basic .NET Programming Environment

To code a program such as the Commission Calculator, you must familiarize yourself with the Visual Basic .NET environment. The environment is called the **Integrated Development Environment (IDE),** and it contains the windows and toolbars that allow you to develop Visual Basic .NET programs. When working on a project in Visual Basic .NET, you should set your monitor to as high a resolution as you can comfortably view, so that you can display multiple windows and toolbars. The screens shown in this book use a 1024 × 768 resolution. For more information about working in the IDE, see Appendix B.

Starting Visual Basic .NET is similar to starting other Windows applications. Because Visual Basic .NET is a part of a suite of programs called Visual Studio .NET, the application that you start is named Visual Studio .NET. The following steps start the Visual Basic .NET application.

1. Click the Start button on the taskbar and then point to All Programs on the Start menu.
2. Point to Microsoft Visual Studio .NET 2003 on the All Programs submenu.
3. Click Microsoft Visual Studio .NET 2003 on the Microsoft Visual Studio .NET 2003 submenu.
4. If necessary, click the Maximize button to maximize the application window.

When you perform the steps above, Visual Basic .NET starts and displays the IDE, as shown in Figure 1-4. The IDE first opens to the Start page, which includes the New Project and Open Project buttons that allow you to start a new project or open an existing project. The Projects page includes a list of projects recently opened. The My Profile tab opens the My Profile page that allows you to customize the IDE in a number of ways. The main work area is the portion of the IDE where you will write code and perform other tasks.

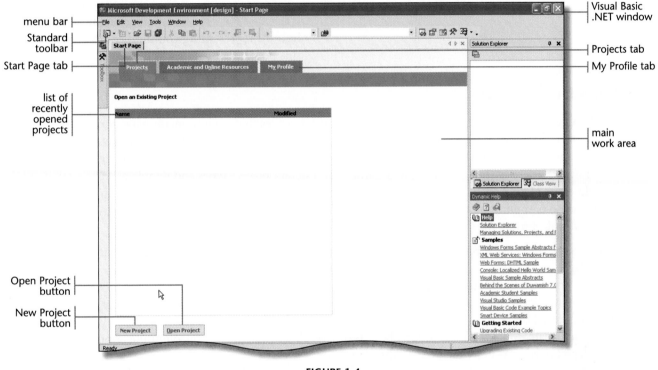

FIGURE 1-4

The **menu bar** displays the Visual Basic .NET menu names, each of which represents a list of commands that allow you to perform essential tasks such as create, edit, save, print, test, and run a Visual Basic .NET application or component. The **Standard toolbar** contains buttons or boxes that execute commonly used commands such as New Project, Save, Cut, Copy, Paste, and others as shown in Figure 1-5.

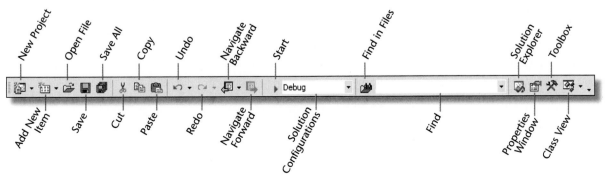

FIGURE 1-5

Decrease
Indent

Comment
out the
selected lines

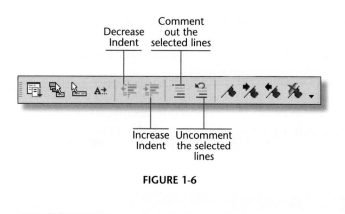

Increase
Indent

Uncomment
the selected
lines

FIGURE 1-6

The Standard toolbar allows you to perform common tasks more quickly than when using menus. For example, to save your work, you can click the Save button on the Standard toolbar instead of clicking File on the menu bar and then clicking Save on the File menu. Each button has a picture, or icon, on the button face to help identify the button's function. Also, when you move the mouse pointer over a button or box, the name of the button or box displays below it in a **ScreenTip**.

Figure 1-6 shows the Text Editor toolbar, which is displayed as you are writing code in the IDE. The buttons representing common commands used in this book are indicated in the figure.

Starting a New Project

As you have learned, a project is a collection of code and other files that usually encompasses one program. When you start Visual Basic .NET, you can choose to open an existing project or start a new project. When you choose to start a new project, you can choose which type of application or Windows component you want to create.

Visual Basic .NET allows you to select from a number of different project types and templates so you can develop many different types of applications. The Commission Calculator program is a Console program. The program is based on the Console Application template provided by Visual Basic .NET. The following steps start Visual Basic .NET and start a new project using the Console Application template.

1. If necessary, start Visual Basic .NET. When the Start Page displays, click the New Project button on the Start Page.
2. If necessary, click the More button in the New Project dialog box.
3. If necessary, click Visual Basic Projects in the Project Types box. If necessary, select Console Application in the Templates box.
4. Click the Create directory for Solution check box. Double-click the text, ConsoleApplication1, in the Name box. Type `CommissionCalculator` in the Name box.
5. Click the Browse button in the New Project dialog box. When the Project Location dialog box is displayed, if necessary, click 3½ Floppy (A:) in the Look in list or select the hard drive and folder for your program. If necessary, click the Create New Folder button on the dialog box toolbar, type `Chapter1` in the Name box and then click the OK button.
6. Click the Open button in the New Project dialog box.
7. Click the OK button. After the new CommissionCalculator project is created, if necessary, click the Maximize button on the Visual Basic .NET title bar to maximize the Visual Basic .NET window.
8. If necessary, click the Module1.vb tab in the main work area.

After the steps above have been performed, the Visual Basic .NET window appears as shown in Figure 1-7. Clicking the Create directory for Solution check box instructs Visual Basic .NET to create a subdirectory with the same names as the project when the project is created.

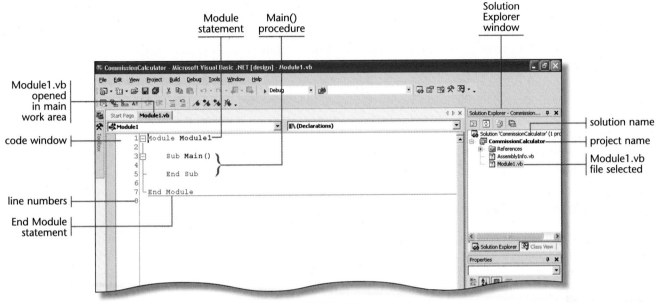

FIGURE 1-7

When a project is opened or created, Visual Basic .NET opens the project within a solution, as shown in Figure 1-7. A **solution** is a grouping of projects and related files. Solutions can contain one project, such as the CommissionCalculator, or many related projects, data files, graphics, and other files. The Solution Explorer window on the right side of the Visual Basic .NET window in Figure 1-7 displays a list of files that were created for the CommissionCalculator project. The Module1.vb file, which will contain the code for the program, is opened in the main work area in a code window. The **code window** provides an area where you can edit and view code. Several lines of code are inserted by Visual Basic .NET automatically when you start a new Console Application project. Line 1 specifies to Visual Basic .NET that this is the start of a new code file, or **module**. Line 7 designates the end of the module. Line 3 indicates the beginning of a section of code known as a procedure. A **procedure** is a section of code that performs a specific task, such as a calculation. A module may contain one or more procedures. All of the code for the CommissionCalculator program will be written in the Main() procedure. When the program executes, Visual Basic .NET automatically executes the Main() procedure first.

Figure 1-7 also shows that line numbers are displayed in the left margin of the main work area. In Visual Basic .NET, the default setting for this option is not to display line numbers. If line numbers are not displayed, the following steps turn on the option to display line numbers in the code window.

1. Click Tools on the menu bar and then click Options.
2. In the Options dialog box, click the Text Editor folder and then click the Basic folder.
3. If necessary, in the Display area, click Line numbers to select it.
4. Click the OK button in the Options dialog box.

The remainder of this book will utilize line numbers when discussing and printing code.

Writing Code

In Visual Basic .NET, the code window includes a built-in technology called IntelliSense to help you write code. **IntelliSense** anticipates your needs during coding and displays prompts to assist you. As you type in the code window, IntelliSense provides assistance by helping to complete words as you type; displaying appropriate list boxes from which you can select events, properties, or methods; and highlighting typographical or syntax errors in your code. A **syntax error** is an error caused by code statements that violate one of the structure or syntax rules of the Visual Basic .NET language.

As shown in Figure 1-2 on page 3, using proper spacing and indentation as you write code in the code window will make the code more readable. The TAB key often is used to align code properly. Using blank spaces also is acceptable, but more cumbersome to enter. Companies or programming teams usually maintain their own set of coding standards that instruct programmers how code should be indented or aligned in the code window. In this book, code is indented and aligned by pressing the TAB key one or more times. By default, the Visual Basic .NET IDE automatically indents the code, based on the lines of code above and below the code being entered.

Adding Comment Statements

Programmers often add comments within their code statements as a form of internal documentation. As discussed earlier, a comment is text added within a section of code that explains how the code works or why it was written. Comments can be included in code as a separate line of code or placed at the end of a line of code. Regardless of their position in the code, comments are not executed when the program is run. Comments are included only for informational purposes for you and for other programmers.

> **Best Practices**
>
> Use comments to remind yourself and other programmers of the purpose of code. Use comments in the following two ways:
>
> 1. Place a comment that identifies the module and its purpose at the top of every file that contains code. This type of comment typically is called a comment header.
> 2. Place comments near portions of code that need clarification or serve an important purpose.

Table 1-2 shows the general form of the comment statement. As shown in Table 1-2, each comment line must begin with an apostrophe (') or the letters REM. Appendix C summarizes all of the general forms of statements introduced in this book.

Table 1-2 Comment Statement

General form:	1. ' comment 2. REM comment 3. code 'comment
Purpose:	To insert explanatory comments in a program as internal documentation.

Examples:	1. ' Chapter 1: Commission Calculator
	   ' Programmer: J. Quasney
	   ' Date: September 7, 2005
	   ' Purpose: This project calculates a salesperson's commissions
	   ' based on a commission percentage, total sales amount,
	   ' and total returns from customers.
	2. REM Calculate the commission
	3. Dim intOpenTickets As Decimal 'Declares variable intOpenTickets

In the code used for the Commission Calculator program, a comment header identifies the program, programmer, date, and purpose for the Commission Calculator program. Figure 1-8 shows the comment header. If line numbers are set to display in the code window, Visual Basic .NET automatically adds the line numbers shown in Figure 1-8.

```
2       ' Chapter 1:     Commission Calculator
3       ' Programmer:    J. Quasney
4       ' Date:          September 7, 2005
5       ' Purpose:       This project calculates a salesperson's commissions
6       '                based on a commission percentage, total sales amount,
7       '                and total returns from customers.
8       '
```

FIGURE 1-8

The TAB key was used to align and indent the code shown in Figure 1-8. For example, in line 2, one tab character exists before the apostrophe (') and a second tab character exists after the 1: and before the words, Commission Calculator. To enter the code shown in Figure 1-8, place the insertion point in line 2, and then, if necessary, press the TAB key to move the insertion point one tab stop to the right. Next, type the code shown in line 2 of Figure 1-8 starting with the apostrophe ('). When you have finished typing line 2, press the ENTER key and continue entering the code. Visual Basic .NET creates new line numbers each time you type a new line of code. Do not press the ENTER key after typing the last line of code in line 8.

> **Best Practices**
>
> Comments should be entered along the way, as you enter program code, rather than at the end. Writing comments as you work helps you clarify the purpose of code for your own reference. After the program is complete, the comments can help you create the program documentation outside of the code.

Variables, Data Types, and Interacting with the User

A **value**, such as 225, 0.05, 78.28, "yes", "no", or the value allowed for the total sales in the Commission Calculator program, is any number, text, or other data that programs use in the code. Variables and constants are used in code statements to store temporary values used by other code statements. A **variable** represents a named location in computer memory that can change values as the code executes. A **constant** also represents a named location in computer memory, but its value cannot change during execution of code. Constants often are used to store values that are used many times in a program. The value assigned to a constant is defined in the program requirements before the program is created.

When you want to use a variable or constant in code, you first must declare the variable or constant. When you **declare** a variable or constant, you tell Visual Basic .NET the name and data type of the variable or constant you want to use. The next sections discuss data types and how to declare variables.

Data Types

The **data type** of a variable or constant determines what kind of data the variable or constant can store. For example, in the Commission Calculator program, the value for total sales is a numeric value. As shown in Table 1-3, Visual Basic .NET supports several data types for character (text) values, such as character and string; several types for numeric values, such as decimal and integer; and several types for other values, such as dates.

Table 1-3 Visual Basic .NET Data Types

CATEGORY	DATA TYPE	DESCRIPTION	RANGE
Character	Char	16-bit (2 bytes) character	1 16-bit character
	String	Sequence of 0 or more 16-bit characters	0 to 2,147,483,647 16-bit characters
Integral	Short	16-bit (2 bytes) integer value	-32,768 to 32,767
	Integer	32-bit (4 bytes) integer value	-2,147,483,648 to 2,147,483,647
	Long	64-bit (8 bytes) integer value	-9,223,372,036,854,775,808 to 9,223,372,036,854,775,807
	Byte	8-bit (1 byte) unsigned integer value	0 to 255
Nonintegral	Decimal	128-bit (16 bytes) fixed point	1.0e-28 to 7.9e28
	Single	32-bit floating point	+-1.5e-45 to +-3.4e38
	Double	64-bit floating point	+-5.0e-324 to +-1.7e308
Miscellaneous	Boolean	32-bit value	True or False
	Date	64-bit signed integer — each increment represents 100 nanoseconds elapsed since the beginning of January 1 in the year 1	January 1, 0001:00:00:00 to December 31, 9999:23:59:59
	Object	32-bit number that represents the location of the object in memory	Any object

As shown in Table 1-3, each data type takes up a certain number of bytes in memory when the variable or constant is used. As you write the code for an application, you choose the data type for variables and constants in code. In general, you should try to use the data type that takes up the smallest amount of memory to ensure the program runs efficiently. In addition, where possible, you should try to use integral data types that represent whole numbers, such as 1, 5, and 1000, because arithmetic operations are fastest with whole numbers. If a variable or constant might contain a decimal, you should use a nonintegral data type. The Decimal data type is recommended when you need to represent currency values.

> **Best Practices**
>
> When selecting the data type to use for a variable or constant, try to use the data type that takes up the smallest amount of memory. Use an integral data type if a variable or constant will not contain a decimal amount; use a nonintegral data type if a variable or constant might contain a decimal; and use a Decimal data type if a variable or constant will contain a currency value.

Declaring Variables

As previously discussed, when you want to use a variable in code, you first must declare the variable by telling Visual Basic .NET the name and data type of the variable. You also can assign an initial value to the variable. For numeric data types, when no initial value is stated, the initial value is 0 by default.

The following rules apply when choosing names for variables and constants.

1. The name can use only letters, numbers, or underscore characters. The name should begin with a letter, although the name can begin with an underscore as long as another valid character also is used in the name.
2. The name can be up to 16,383 characters in length.
3. The name cannot contain punctuation, special characters (other than the underscore character), or blank spaces.

When naming variables, a common practice among programmers is to use standard prefixes for the variable name in order to indicate the data type of the variable. For example, a decimal variable for the total sales amount in the Commission Calculator program may be named *decSales* to indicate that the variable is of the Decimal data type. Table 1-4 shows the prefixes used for naming variables in this book, based on their data type.

The Dim statement is used to declare a variable. Table 1-5 shows the general form of a Dim statement.

Table 1-4 Naming Convention for Variables

DATA TYPE	PREFIX
Short	shr
Integer	int
Long	lng
Byte	byt
Decimal	dec
Single	sng
Double	dbl
Char	chr
String	str
Boolean	bln
Date	dtm
Object	obj

Table 1-5 Dim Statement

General form:	1. Dim variablename As datatype = initialvalue 2. Dim variablename As datatype 3. Dim variablename, variablename As datatype 4. Dim variablename
Purpose:	The Dim statement declares and/or intializes a variable, where variablename can be the name of a variable.
Examples:	1. Dim intPeopleCount As Integer = 100 2. Dim decCommission As Decimal 3. Dim decSales, decReturns As Decimal 4. Dim lngInStock

Figure 1-9 shows the code that declares variables necessary for the Commission Calculator program. The code declares three variables: *decSales*, *decReturns*, and *decCommission*. All of the variables are of the Decimal data type because the Decimal data type is the preferred data type to use when working with currency values. The *decSales* variable will hold the value of the total sales entered by the user. The *decReturns* variable will hold the value of the total returns entered by the user. Finally, the *decCommission* variable will be assigned the resulting commission that is calculated and displayed as the program's output.

```
10        Dim decSales, decReturns As Decimal
11        Dim decCommission As Decimal
```

FIGURE 1-9

To enter the code shown in Figure 1-9, place the insertion point in line 10 below the Sub Main() code in line 9 in the code window. Enter the code as shown in Figure 1-9, pressing the ENTER key after each line. Line 12 will be a blank line.

> **Best Practices**
>
> When naming variables, use names that describe the purpose of the variable, such as decSales to store a decimal value for sales numbers or intAvailSeats to store an integer value for the number of seats available on a flight. Using descriptive names helps clarify the purpose of the variable and makes the code easier to understand.

Writing to the Console Window

Before accepting the total sales amount from the user as an input value, a message requesting the input must be displayed to the user, so that the user knows to enter the input data. Because the Commission Calculator program is a Console program, the program code must interact with the Console window to display prompts, accept inputs, and then display output. Figure 1-10 shows a comment line and a line of code that causes a message to be displayed in the Console window. The code in line 14 is a **method**, which is a type of instruction that tells the program to manipulate values, generate outputs, or perform actions. Visual Basic .NET includes an extensive library of methods that you can use to perform actions for you in your code. When the **Console.Write() method** executes, the text in quotes within the parentheses is displayed in the Console window and the insertion point is positioned at the end of the text.

```
13          ' Accept the total sales and total returns from the Console window
14          Console.Write("Please enter the total sales in dollars: ")
```

FIGURE 1-10

To enter the code shown in Figure 1-10, place the insertion point in line 12 (a blank line) and then press the ENTER key. Enter the code as shown in Figure 1-10, pressing the ENTER key after each line.

Assignment Statements

The **assignment statement** is used to assign the desired value to a variable. The general form of the code statement used to change the value of a variable is

variable = newvalue

where variable is the name of the variable and newvalue is the new value to which the variable should be changed. The assignment statement tells the application to set the variable on the left side of the statement to the value on the right side of the statement. This value may be a constant, data input by the user, or the result of an **expression**, which is a statement that performs a calculation, manipulates characters, or tests data. In the Commission Calculator application, for example, you can use an assignment statement to change the *decSales* variable when the program executes, so that it contains the total sales value entered by the user. Table 1-6 shows the general form of the assignment statement.

Table 1-6 Assignment Statement	
General form:	1. variable = newvalue 2. variable = result of expression
Purpose:	To change the value of the variable on the left side of the equal sign to the value on the right side of the equal sign.
Examples:	1. `i = 0` 2. `decCommission = 0.14 * (decTotalSales - decTotalReturns)` 3. `intCount = intCount + 1` 4. `intInventory = intInventory - 1` 5. `decAverage = decSum / decCount`

Reading Input from the Console Window

Just as you write information to the Console window, you also can read data input by the user from the Console window. The **Console.ReadLine() method** reads all of the data input by the user until the user presses the ENTER key. The Console.ReadLine() method can be placed on the right side of an assignment statement so that you can assign the data entered by the user to a variable on the left side of the assignment statement. Figure 1-11 shows the code for reading data using the Console.ReadLine() method and assigning the data entered by the user to the *decSales* variable.

```
15          decSales = Console.ReadLine()
```

FIGURE 1-11

The code in Figure 1-11 executes after the code shown in Figure 1-10 displays the input prompt to the user. After the user types a value and then presses the ENTER key, the code in Figure 1-11 executes. The value entered by the user is read from the Console window and then the value is assigned to the *decSales* variable. The *decSales* variable contains the value and will continue to contain that value until the value is changed by another line of code or the program terminates.

Before calculating the commission due on the value stored in the *decSales* variable, the program requires that the total returns be entered by the user. Figure 1-12 shows the code necessary to display a prompt to the user, read the total returns value entered by the user, and then assign the value to the *decReturns* variable. The code in Figure 1-12 executes after the user has entered the total sales.

```
16          Console.Write("Please enter the total returns in dollars: ")
17          decReturns = Console.ReadLine()
```

FIGURE 1-12

The code shown in Figures 1-11 and 1-12 should be entered in the CommissionCalculator code window just after line 14. After entering the code, press the ENTER key to create a blank line on line 18.

Numeric Expressions and Operator Precedence

As you have learned, an expression is used to perform calculations, manipulate characters, or test data. A **numeric expression** is any expression that can be evaluated as a number. A numeric expression can include values, variables, and constants. The data type of any value in a numeric expression must be one of the numeric data types from Table 1-3 on page 10. A numeric expression cannot contain string variables or string values.

The values, variables, and constants in a numeric expression often are separated from each other by parentheses and arithmetic operators. An **arithmetic operator** is used to manipulate two or more numeric values. Commonly used arithmetic operators are the plus sign (+), which is used to add, or sum, two numbers; and the asterisk (*), which is used to multiply two numbers. Table 1-7 shows seven arithmetic operators listed in the order of operator precedence. **Order of operator precedence** is a predetermined order that defines the sequence in which operators are evaluated and resolved when several operations occur in an expression.

Table 1-7 Arithmetic Operators

ARITHMETIC OPERATOR	MEANING
^	Raise a number to the power of an exponent
*	Multiply two numbers
/	Divide two numbers and return a decimal result
\	Divide two numbers and return an integer result
Mod	Divide two numbers and return only the remainder as an integer
+	Sum two numbers
−	Find the difference between two numbers or to indicate the negative value of a numeric expression

The process of raising a number to the power of an exponent is called exponentiation. For example, $5 \wedge 2$ is the same as 5^2 and is equal to 25, and $6 \wedge 3$ is the same as 6^3 and is equal to 216. In programming, the asterisk (*) is used to indicate multiplication and the forward slash (/) indicates division. Therefore, 8 * 5 is equal to 40, and 10 / 2 is equal to 5. For addition and subtraction, the traditional + and − signs are used.

Two arithmetic operators that may be unfamiliar are the backslash (\) and Mod, both of which are used to indicate a division operation. The backslash operator instructs Visual Basic .NET first to round the dividend and the divisor to integers (whole numbers) and then truncate any decimal portion of the quotient. For example, 5 \ 3 is equal to 1 because 5 divided by 3 is 1.6666, which is truncated to the integer 1; and 6.8 \ 3.2 is equal to 2 because 6.8 divided by 3.2 is rounded to 6 divided by 3, which is 2.

The **Mod operator** (also called the **modulo operator**) is used to divide two numbers and then return the remainder of the division operation as an integer. For example, 44 Mod 6 is equal to 2 because 44 divided by 6 is 7 with a remainder of 2. Also, 27 Mod 12 is equal to 3 because 27 divided by 12 is 2 with a remainder of 3.

Writing Valid Expressions

For an expression to be considered validly formed, an arithmetic operator must be included between each operand. For example, the following statement formed to assign *A* twice the value of *B* is invalid:

```
A = 2B    ' Invalid statement
```

Visual Basic .NET will reject the statement because a value and a variable within the same expression must be separated by an arithmetic operator. The statement can be written validly as follows:

```
A = 2 * B
```

It also is invalid to use a string variable or string constant in a numeric expression. String values are placed within double quotes in code. The following are invalid numeric expressions:

```
6 + "SALES" / C       'Invalid statement
"25" / B + "X" - 19   'Invalid statement
```

Order of Operations

As you form complex numeric expressions involving several arithmetic operations, it is important to consider the order in which Visual Basic .NET will evaluate the expression. For example, if you entered

```
A = 24 / 4 / 2
```

as an expression, would the expression assign a value of 3 or 12 to *A*? The answer depends on how Visual Basic .NET evaluates the expression. If Visual Basic .NET completes the operation 24 / 4 first and only then 6 / 2, the expression yields the value 3. If Visual Basic .NET completes the second operation 4 / 2 first and only then 24 / 2, it yields 12.

Visual Basic .NET follows the normal algebraic rules to evaluate an expression. The normal algebraic rules that define the order in which the operations are evaluated are as follows: unless parentheses dictate otherwise, reading from left to right in a numeric expression, all exponentiations are performed first, then all multiplications and/or divisions, then all integer divisions, then all modulo arithmetic, and finally, all additions and/or subtractions. Following these algebraic rules, Visual Basic .NET would evaluate the expression 24 / 4 / 2 to yield a value of 3.

This order of operator precedence, which defines the order in which operators are evaluated, sometimes is called the rules of precedence or the hierarchy of operations. The meaning of these rules can be made clear with some examples.

For example, the expression 18 / 3 ^ 2 + 4 * 2 is evaluated as follows:

```
A = 18 / 3 ^ 2 + 4 * 2
A = 18 / 9 + 4 * 2
A = 2 + 8
A = 10
```

If you have trouble following the logic behind this evaluation, use the following technique. Whenever a numeric expression is to be evaluated, read or scan the expression from left to right five different times and apply the order of operator precedence rules outlined above each time you read the expression. On the first scan, every time you encounter an ^ operator, you perform exponentiation. In this example, 3 is raised to the power of 2, yielding 9.

On the second scan, moving from left to right again, every time you encounter the operators, * and /, perform multiplication and division. Hence, 18 is divided by 9, yielding 2; and 4 and 2 are multiplied, yielding 8. On the third scan, from left to right, perform all integer division. On the fourth scan, from left to right, perform all modulo arithmetic. This example includes no integer division or modulo arithmetic so no operations are performed. On the fifth scan, moving again from left to right, every time you encounter the operators, + and –, perform addition and subtraction. In this example, 2 and 8 are added to form 10.

The following expression includes all seven arithmetic operators and yields a value of 2.

```
A = 3 * 9 Mod 2 ^ 2 + 5 \ 4.8 / 2 - 3
A = 3 * 9 Mod 4 + 5 \ 4.8 / 2 - 3   ◄————————end of first scan
A = 27 Mod 4 + 5 \ 2.4 - 3  ◄————————end of second scan
A = 27 Mod 4 + 2 - 3 ◄————————end of third scan
A = 3 + 2 - 3 ◄————————end of fourth scan
A = 2 ◄————————end of fifth scan
```

When operations of the same precedence are encountered, the normal rules of precedence apply. For example, when evaluated left to right:

```
A - B - C is interpreted as (A - B) - C
A / B / C is interpreted as (A / B) / C
A ^ B ^ C is interpreted as (A ^ B) ^ C
A \ B \ C is interpreted as (A \ B) \ C
A Mod B Mod C is interpreted as (A Mod B) Mod C
```

Using Parentheses in Numeric Expressions

Parentheses may be used to change the order of operations. In Visual Basic .NET, parentheses normally are used to avoid ambiguity and to group terms in a numeric expression. The order in which the operations in an expression containing parentheses are evaluated can be stated as follows: when parentheses are inserted into an expression, the part of the expression within the parentheses is evaluated first, and then the remaining expression is evaluated according to the normal order of operator precedence.

If the first example was rewritten with parentheses, as A = (18 / 3) ^ 2 + 4 * 2, then it would be evaluated in the following manner:

```
A = (18 / 3) ^ 2 + 4 * 2
A = 6 ^ 2 + 4 * 2
A = 36 + 4 * 2
A = 36 + 8
A = 44
```

Evaluating expressions with parentheses should be done as follows: Make five scans from left to right within each pair of parentheses, and only after doing this, make the standard five passes over the entire numeric expression.

The expression below yields the value of 1.41, as follows:

```
A = (2 - 3 * 4 / 5) ^ 2 + 5 / (4 * 3 - 2 ^ 3)
A = (2 - 3 * 4 / 5) ^ 2 + 5 / (4 * 3 - 8)
A = (2 - 2.4) ^ 2 + 5 / (12 - 8)
A = (-0.4) ^ 2 + 5 / 4
A = 0.16 + 5 / 4
A = 0.16 + 1.25
A = 1.41
```

When coding a numeric expression, use parentheses freely when in doubt as to the valid form and evaluation of a numeric expression. For example, if you want Visual Basic .NET to divide 8 * D by 3 ^ P, the expression may be written correctly as A = 8 * D / 3 ^ P, but you also may write it as follows:

```
A = (8 * D) / (3 ^ P)
```

For more complex expressions, Visual Basic .NET allows parentheses to be contained within other parentheses. When this occurs, the parentheses are said to be nested. In this case, Visual Basic .NET evaluates the innermost parenthetical expression first and then goes on to the next innermost parenthetical expression, until the expression is evaluated completely.

Best Practices

When coding a numeric expression, use parentheses freely when in doubt as to the valid form and evaluation of a numeric expression. Adding parentheses helps to provide clarity when you are writing code or a program is evaluating an expression.

Coding the Expression for the Commission Calculator

Figure 1-13 shows the code necessary to compute the commission due to a salesperson based on total sales and total returns. Parentheses are used to make certain that the computation of the commission first subtracts the total returns from the total sales before multiplying by the commission rate. The resulting value from the expression is assigned to the *decCommission* variable. After the line of code executes, the *decCommission* variable contains the commission value that can be displayed to the user.

```
19          ' Calculate the commission
20          decCommission = 0.14 * (decSales - decReturns)
```

FIGURE 1-13

Once the commission is calculated, the Console.WriteLine() method can be used to display the resulting commission to the user. The **Console.WriteLine() method** operates in a manner similar to the Console.Write() method, but additionally starts a new line after writing information to the Console window. If no information is given to the Console.WriteLine() method within the parentheses, then a blank line is written to the Console window. Writing blank lines to the Console window is a good way of making the output displayed in the window more readable.

Figure 1-14 shows the remaining code for the Commission Calculator program. Line 23 writes a blank line to the Console window. Lines 24 and 25 use the Console.WriteLine() method to write information to the Console window. The information in the parentheses in line 24 uses the **string concatenation (&) operator** to join two pieces of information — in this example, a description of the value and the value in the *decCommission* variable. When the code executes, the string, The commission is, is combined with the value in the *decCommission* variable to create an output message for the user. The Console.WriteLine() method then places the resulting string in the Console window and then starts a new line in the window.

Line 26 uses the **Console.Read() method** to wait for the user to press a key before the program exits. If the Console.Read() method was excluded, then the program would exit after line 25 executed and the Console window automatically would close, without giving the user time to see the output value. After the Console.Read() method receives any keystroke from the user on the keyboard, then the final statement in the program — the End Sub statement — executes, the program halts, and the Console window closes.

```
22          ' Write the results to the Console window
23          Console.WriteLine()
24          Console.WriteLine("The commission is " & decCommission)
25          Console.WriteLine("Press any key to continue.")
26          Console.Read()
```

FIGURE 1-14

The code shown in Figures 1-13 and 1-14 should be entered in the Commission Calculator code window after line 18 (a blank line). As shown in Figure 1-15 on the next page, a blank line is added in line 21 in order to make the code more readable. Figure 1-15 shows the complete code for the Commission Calculator program. After both segments of code are added to the program, the coding for the Commission Calculator program is complete and the program can be saved and tested.

```
 1 Module Module1
 2     ' Chapter 1:      Commission Calculator
 3     ' Programmer:     J. Quasney
 4     ' Date:           September 7, 2005
 5     ' Purpose:        This project calculates a salesperson's commissions
 6     '                 based on a commission percentage, total sales amount,
 7     '                 and total returns from customers.
 8     '
 9     Sub Main()
10         Dim decSales, decReturns As Decimal
11         Dim decCommission As Decimal
12
13         ' Accept the total sales and total returns from the Console window
14         Console.Write("Please enter the total sales in dollars: ")
15         decSales = Console.ReadLine()
16         Console.Write("Please enter the total returns in dollars: ")
17         decReturns = Console.ReadLine()
18
19         ' Calculate the commission
20         decCommission = 0.14 * (decSales - decReturns)
21
22         ' Write the results to the Console window
23         Console.WriteLine()
24         Console.WriteLine("The commission is " & decCommission)
25         Console.WriteLine("Press any key to continue.")
26         Console.Read()
27     End Sub
28
29 End Module
```

FIGURE 1-15

Saving, Testing, and Documenting the Program

Before starting a new Visual Basic .NET project or quitting Visual Basic .NET, you should save your work. You also should save your project periodically while you are working on it and before you run it for the first time. Visual Basic .NET will save your project automatically when you run it. During the process of developing a project, however, you should err on the side of caution and save your work often.

Best Practices

You should save your work periodically while you are working on a project and again before you run the project. Make backups of your work that you can store in a separate physical location.

Saving a Project

Visual Basic .NET projects are saved as a set of files that include the program code and other information about the project. For example, one of the files used extensively in the Commission Calculator project is the Module1.vb file, which is indicated on the tab in the main work area (Figure 1-7 on page 7). The Module1.vb file contains the code shown in this chapter. Other files saved with a project contain information about the type of project and other options that are saved with the project.

Clicking the Save All button on the Standard toolbar saves all files associated with a project. Clicking the Save button saves only the current file you are working on in the main work area. Using the Save button is practical if you are modifying an individual file that is part of a much larger project. If you want to save your work with a different file name or in a different folder or drive, click the Save Module1.vb As command on the File menu. The File menu also contains both a Save and Save All command that function just as the buttons on the Standard toolbar.

Running a Visual Basic .NET Application

Once the project is saved, you should run the project to test that your code functions as intended. You also should test changes frequently as you are working on a project. If you have several changes to make to a program, for instance, it is important to test each change individually, so you easily can identify which change introduced a new problem into the project. The Visual Basic .NET IDE allows you to run projects in order to test the functionality of programs that you develop. When you run a project, the project is loaded into memory and the program code is executed by the .NET architecture. By running your projects often during the coding phase, you can check for any problems, or **bugs**, that you may have introduced into your code inadvertently.

As previously discussed, an application is the version of your project that you distribute to end users. In the case of the Commission Calculator program, the application consists of an executable file named CommisssionCalculator.exe. The .exe file extension indicates that the file is an executable file. When users run your application, they will not need to use the Visual Basic .NET IDE.

When you run a project, the IDE enters a mode called **run time**. When run time begins, the IDE changes significantly, closing some windows and opening others. The functionality of some of these new windows is discussed in Appendix B. To run the program, click the Start button on the Standard toolbar, as shown in Figure 1-16. As the program begins to run, Visual Basic .NET opens several windows. The word, [design], on the Visual Basic .NET title bar changes to [run]. A Console window opens and the first prompt is presented on the first line of the window. Type in data to test the program, pressing the ENTER key after each entry. After entering the total returns, the program displays the results (Figure 1-16).

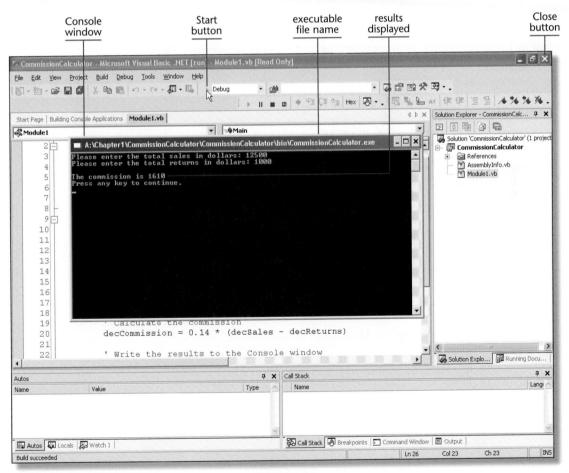

FIGURE 1-16

After running the program and testing one set of data, you can click the Start button to run the application again and then use different data values for the total sales and total returns. As just mentioned, running your projects allows you to check for bugs introduced into your code and verify that the project displays and behaves correctly. Running a project also enables you to learn about the program before you make modifications to it.

Printing the Code and the Console Window

A printed record, also called a **hard copy output**, can make it easier to check your program or refine it. Often, project requirements dictate that you archive a hard copy output of an application's code to share with a client or other developers.

Visual Basic .NET includes functionality that allows you to print a hard copy of the code used in a project. The Print command is available on the File menu when the active window contains printable items, such as code, Help topics, Web pages, or other printable output. Before printing the code, check if line numbers will print with the code by clicking File on the menu bar and then clicking Page Setup. If necessary, click Line numbers to select it and then click the OK button in the Page Setup dialog box. Then, to print the Commission Calculator program code, make certain that the code is displayed in the main work area and that the insertion point is positioned within the code window. You then can print the code by clicking File on the menu bar and then clicking Print on the File menu.

Figure 1-17 shows the resulting code listing. If a line of code is too long to fit on one line of the printout, then the line will include a continuation marker on the right side of the page. A **continuation marker** indicates that a line of code was too long to print on one line and is continued on the next line. Because the lines of code in this program are relatively short, the printout shown in Figure 1-17 does not show any continuation markers.

```
A:\Chapter1\CommissionCalculator\CommissionCalculator\Module1.vb                          1
 1  Module Module1
 2      ' Chapter 1:      Commission Calculator
 3      ' Programmer:     J. Quasney
 4      ' Date:           September 7, 2005
 5      ' Purpose:        This project calculates a salesperson's commissions
 6      '                 based on a commission percentage, total sales amount,
 7      '                 and total returns from customers.
 8      '
 9      Sub Main()
10          Dim decSales, decReturns As Decimal
11          Dim decCommission As Decimal
12
13          ' Accept the total sales and total returns from the Console window
14          Console.Write("Please enter the total sales in dollars: ")
15          decSales = Console.ReadLine()
16          Console.Write("Please enter the total returns in dollars: ")
17          decReturns = Console.ReadLine()
18
19          ' Calculate the commission
20          decCommission = 0.14 * (decSales - decReturns)
21
22          ' Write the results to the Console window
23          Console.WriteLine()
24          Console.WriteLine("The commission is " & decCommission)
25          Console.WriteLine("Press any key to continue.")
26          Console.Read()
27      End Sub
28
29  End Module
30
```

FIGURE 1-17

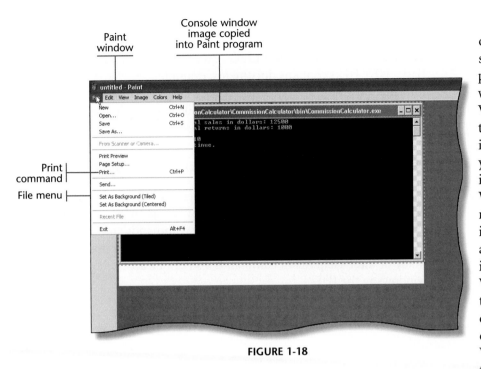

FIGURE 1-18

In addition to printing a copy of the program's code, you also should print a copy of the program interface of the Console window during run time. While Visual Basic .NET includes functionality to print code, it does not include functionality that allows you to print the application while it is running; you must use other Windows capabilities to print a record of the application while it is running. One easy way to print a copy of the running application is to press ALT+PRTSCR to use Windows' built-in ability to capture the contents of the screen display. After the screen image is captured, it can be pasted into the Windows Paint application and then printed.

The following steps print a record of the Console window while the Commission Calculator program is running.

1. In the Visual Basic .NET window, click the Start button on the Standard toolbar to run the Commission Calculator program.
2. Enter the two input values as requested by the prompts.
3. When the computer displays the result, press ALT+PRTSCR (the PRINT SCREEN key) to capture an image of the Console window.
4. Click the Start button on the Windows taskbar, point to All Programs on the Start menu, point to Accessories on the All Programs submenu, and then click Paint on the Accessories submenu.
5. When the Paint window opens, click Edit on the menu bar.
6. Click Paste on the Edit menu.
7. Click File on the menu bar (Figure 1-18).
8. Click Print on the File menu.
9. Click the Print button in the Print dialog box.
10. Click the Close button on the Paint window title bar. When the Paint dialog box is displayed to confirm whether you want to save the pasted image, click the No button.

The resulting printout should show the Commission Calculator program as shown in Figure 1-16 on page 19. In addition to pasting the copied screen image into Paint, you also can paste the screen images into programs such as Microsoft Word or Microsoft PowerPoint. Additionally, you can save an electronic version of the screen in Paint by using the Save As command on the File menu in the Paint program.

Quitting Visual Basic .NET

When you have completed working with Visual Basic .NET, you should quit the Visual Basic .NET system to conserve memory for other Windows applications. To quit Visual Basic .NET, click the Visual Basic .NET Close button on the right side of the title bar (Figure 1-16). If you made changes to the project since the last time it was saved, Visual Basic .NET displays a dialog box that asks you if you want to save your work. Click the Yes button to save the changes and then close Visual Basic .NET, click the No button to close Visual Basic .NET without saving the changes, or click the Cancel button to return to Visual Basic .NET without saving the changes. Clicking the Help button displays information from the Help system.

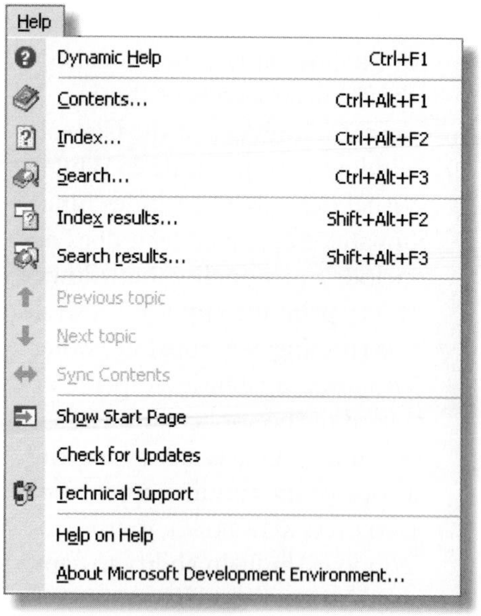

Using Help

The Visual Basic .NET IDE includes an extensive Help system. Visual Basic .NET **Help** contains documents, examples, articles, and other information about the Visual Basic .NET language and environment to assist you in using Visual Basic .NET. While working in the Visual Basic .NET IDE, you can access Help in a number of ways.

Navigating the Visual Basic .NET Help System

As shown in Figure 1-19, the Help menu in the Visual Basic .NET IDE includes a number of commands you can use to access Help.

Table 1-8 summarizes the Help menu commands and where each command displays the Help information by default within the IDE. Many of these Help menu commands also can be accessed using tabs on windows in the IDE.

FIGURE 1-19

Table 1-8 Help Menu Commands

MENU ITEM	DEFAULT DISPLAY AREA	ACTION
Dynamic Help	Lower-right window	Displays the Dynamic Help area.
Contents	Upper-right window	Displays a tree structure of all Help topics.
Index	Upper-right window	Displays an alphabetical list of all Help items.
Search	Upper-right window	Displays a search form that allows you to find topics by entering keywords.
Index results	Lower window	Displays a list of Help articles from an item that is clicked in the Help Index window.
Search results	Lower window	Displays a list of Help articles generated from using the Help Search window.
Previous topic	Main work area	When viewing Help articles in the main work area, allows navigation to the previous Help article that was displayed.
Next topic	Main work area	When viewing Help articles, navigates to the next topic in the Search results window or Index results window.
Sync Contents	Main work area	Causes the Help Contents window to navigate to the item currently being accessed in the Help system.
Show Start Page	Main work area	Displays the initial Visual Basic .NET Start page.
Check for Updates	New window	Attempts to connect to Microsoft's Web site to check for new updates to the Visual Basic .NET application.
Technical Support	Main work area	Displays links where Microsoft technical support can be reached.
Help on Help	Main work area	Displays information on how to get the most out of using the Help system.
About Microsoft Development Environment	New window	Displays copyright information, licensing information, and system information.

Using the Contents, Index, and Search commands typically results in a list of related Help topics. For example, when a user clicks the Search button in the Search window, the Help system searches for Help topics related to the search term. Once it locates topics related to the search term entered in the Search window, it then displays the results in the Search Results window. Double-clicking a topic in the Search Results window displays the Help topic in the main work area, as shown in Figure 1-20.

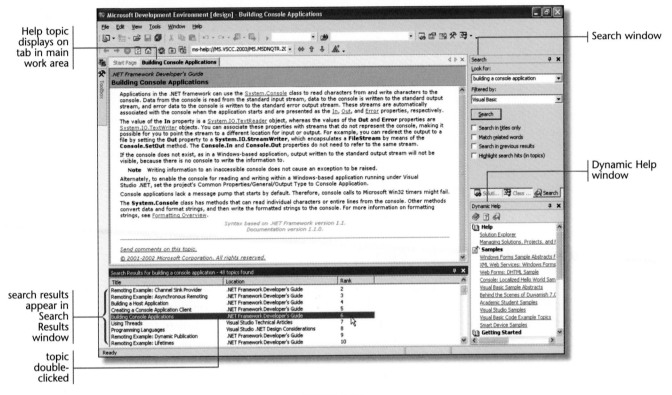

FIGURE 1-20

In Visual Basic .NET, **Dynamic Help** displays Help information for whatever task or window you are working with in the IDE. As you navigate in the IDE, open new windows, or select items on a form, Dynamic Help automatically updates itself with relevant information. By default, the Dynamic Help window opens in the lower-right window in the IDE. You can access Dynamic Help either by clicking the Dynamic Help tab next to the Properties tab in the Properties window or by clicking Dynamic Help on the Help menu.

Chapter Summary

In this chapter, you learned how to design, create, and run a Visual Basic .NET Console program. You also learned the fundamentals of the Visual Basic .NET integrated development environment and how to write code. You learned how to enter code with comments to document the purpose of code. You learned how to declare variables and constants and how data types are used. You also learned how to code numeric expressions and about the order of operator precedence. Finally, you learned how to save, test, and document a program and use the Visual Basic .NET Help tools.

Key Terms

algorithm (4)
application (1)
arithmetic operator (14)
assignment statement (12)
Boolean (10)
bugs (19)
Byte (10)
Char (10)
code window (7)
comment (4)
Console window (3)
Console.Read() method (17)
Console.ReadLine() method (13)
Console.Write() method (12)
Console.WriteLine() method (17)
constant (9)
continuation marker (20)
data type (10)
Date (10)
debugging (2)
Decimal (10)
declare (9)
development cycle (2)

Double (10)
Dynamic Help (23)
execute (3)
expression (12)
flowchart (4)
hard copy output (20)
Help (22)
Integer (10)
Integrated Development
    Environment (IDE) (4)
IntelliSense (8)
keyword (4)
Long (10)
menu bar (5)
method (12)
methodology (2)
Microsoft Visual Basic .NET (1)
Mod operator (14)
module (7)
modulo operator (14)
numeric expression (14)
Object (10)
order of operator precedence (14)

procedure (7)
program (1)
program development (1)
programmer (1)
programming (1)
project (1)
requirements document (2)
run (3)
run time (19)
ScreenTip (6)
Short (10)
Single (10)
software developer (1)
solution (7)
Standard toolbar (5)
String (10)
string concatenation (&) operator
    (17)
syntax error (8)
value (9)
variable (9)

Homework Assignments

Short Answer

1. Which arithmetic operation is performed first in the following numeric expressions?

    a. 12 / 4 * 6

    b. *intPopulation1 + intPopulation2 – intOverlap*

    c. 12 * (*intInventoryAmount* + 100)

    d. (*A* * (6 / *B*)) ^ 8 + (*C* ^ (4 ^ 2)) + 9 Mod 4

    e. (*B* ^ 2 – 4 * *A* * *C*) / (2 * *A*)

    f. *decCost / decInventory + decOverhead*

2. Evaluate each of the following:

    a. 7 * 8 * 2 / 8 – 3 ^ 3 / 9

    b. (5 ^ 3) + 8 * 3

    c. 3 * 6 / 3 + 8 Mod 4 + 7

3. Calculate the numeric value for each of the following valid numeric expressions if $A = 6.0$, $C = 4.0$, $W = 2.0$, $T = 3.0$, $X = 2.0$, and $Y = 2.0$.

    a. $(C - A * 3) + 5.4$

    b. $(A / (C + 1) * 8 - 6) / 2 + (6 \text{ Mod } 4 \setminus 3)$

    c. $60.0 / (X * Y) \wedge W$

    d. $X + 8.0 * Y * W / 4.0 - 8.0 / (T - X / Y) + W \wedge T$

4. Repeat the above assignment for the case of $A = 4.0$, $C = 6.0$, $W = 3.0$, $T = 3.0$, $X = 1.0$, and $Y = 2.0$.

5. Which of the following are invalid variable names in Visual Basic .NET? Why?

    a. *Y*

    b. *int(Currency*

    c. *Dim*

    d. *YT.8*

    e. *4854*

    f. *_Bln*

    g. *_Decimal*

    h. *A-Z*

    i. *QuAnTiTy*

    j. *U10*

6. Write a valid Visual Basic .NET statement for each of the following algebraic statements. Use appropriate variable names.

    a. $a = (x - y)^{1/6}$

    b. $j = 50 - (2/3)^{100} + K^2$

    c. $y = a1x + a2x^2 + a3x^3 + a4x^4$

    d. $Q = (R^3 + S^2)^{3.2}$

7. If necessary, insert parentheses so that each numeric expression results in the value indicated on the right side of the arrow.

    a. 9 / 2 + 1 + 8 —> 11

    b. 9 ^ 4 – 3 —> 9

    c. 9.0 / 6.0 + 0.5 + 6.0 ^ 1.0 —> 8.0

    d. 15 – 3 – 6 – 2 – 3 —> 19

    e. 4 * 3 – 5 * 3 * 2 + 3 —> 105

8. Consider the valid code below. What is displayed in the Console window when the code is executed?

   a.
   ```
   Dim X As Decimal = 3.0
   Dim Y as Decimal = 4.0
   Dim Z as Decimal
   Z = (X ^ 4.0 / X * Y) - (8.0 * Y / 4.0)
   Z = Z + 3.0
   Console.WriteLine(Z)
   ```

   b.
   ```
   Dim X As Decimal = 3.0
   Dim Y As Decimal = 4.0
   Dim W1, W2, W3 As Decimal
   Y = 5.0
   W1 = X * Y
   W3 = 2.0 + 1.0
   W2 = W1 / W3
   X = E1 - E2
   Console.WriteLine(X)
   ```

9. What is written to the Console window after the following code executes?

   ```
   dblAverage1 = 7.0 + 8.0 + 9.0 + 10.0 + 11.0 + 12.0 / 6.0
   dblAverage2 = (7.0 + 8.0 + 9.0 + 10.0 + 11.0 + 12.0) / 6.0
   Console.WriteLine("The average1 is " & dblAverage1)
   Console.Write("The average2 is " & dblAverage2)
   ```

10. Briefly explain how you print code in Visual Basic .NET and capture and print a Console window.

Learn It Online

Instructions: To complete the Learn It Online exercises, start your browser, click the Address bar, and then enter the Web address scsite.com/progvb/learn. When the Programming Fundamentals Learn It Online page is displayed, follow the instructions in the exercises below. Each exercise has instructions for printing your results, either for your own records or for submission to your instructor.

1. **Chapter Reinforcement True/False, Multiple Choice, and Short Answer**   Below Chapter 1, click the Chapter Reinforcement link. Print the quiz by clicking Print on the File menu for each page. Answer each question.

2. **Practice Test**   Below Chapter 1, click the Practice Test link. Answer each question, enter your first and last name at the bottom of the page, and then click the Grade Test button. When the graded practice test is displayed on your screen, click Print on the File menu to print a hard copy. Continue to take practice tests until you score 80% or better.

3. **Crossword Puzzle Challenge**   Below Chapter 1, click the Crossword Puzzle Challenge link. Read the instructions, and then enter your first and last name. Click the SUBMIT button. Work the crossword puzzle. When you are finished, click the Submit button. When the crossword puzzle is redisplayed, click the Print Puzzle button to print a hard copy.

4. **Tips and Tricks**   Below Chapter 1, click the Tips and Tricks link. Click a topic that pertains to Chapter 1. Right-click the information and then click Print on the shortcut menu. Construct a brief example of what the information relates to in Visual Basic .NET to confirm you understand how to use the tip or trick.

5. **Newsgroups**   Below Chapter 1, click the Newsgroups link. Click a topic that pertains to Chapter 1. Print three comments.

6. **Expanding Your Horizons**   Below Chapter 1, click the Expanding Your Horizons link. Click a topic that pertains to Chapter 1. Print the information. Construct a brief example of what the information relates to in Visual Basic .NET to confirm you understand the contents of the article.

7. **Search Sleuth**   Below Chapter 1, click the Search Sleuth link. To search for a term that pertains to this chapter, select a term below the Chapter 1 title and then use the Google search engine at google.com (or any major search engine) to display and print two Web pages that present information on the term.

Programming Assignments

1 Sales Tax Calculation

Marie's Flower Shop would like to provide its front counter employees with a program that calculates the sales tax. The application should let the employee enter the amount of the customer's order and then calculate a 6% sales tax. After the employee enters the order amount and presses the ENTER key, the program should display the amount of the customer's order and the tax, followed by the total of the customer's order and tax added together. For example, an order amount of $100 should result in a tax of $6 and a total of $106 as shown in Figure 1-21.

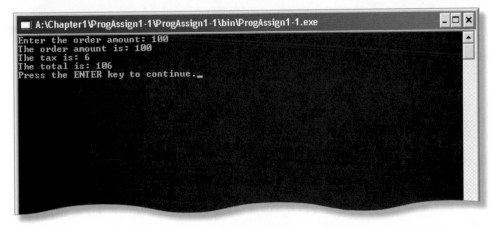

FIGURE 1-21

2 Rule of Thumb Calculation

Your friend is a tailor and performs rule-of-thumb calculations of various types to compute measurements of male customers. These rules are: Neck Size = 3 × (Weight / Waistline), Hat Size = (3 × Weight) / (2.125 × Waistline), and Shoe Size = 50 × (Waistline / Weight). He has asked you to create a Console program that will accept the required inputs, perform the various calculations, and output the results. Use the Decimal data type to represent the values in your code. Be sure to use proper input prompts and output labels. For example, a weight of 120 pounds and a waistline of 30 inches should result in a neck size of 12, a hat size of 6, and a shoe size of 12 as shown in Figure 1-22.

FIGURE 1-22

3 Modulo Operator

Write a program that will write the number of dollars and cents to the Console window based on user numeric input. For instance, if the user inputs 765, the program will write the following to the Console window as shown in Figure 1-23:

Dollars = 7
Cents = 65

FIGURE 1-23

For this program, use integer arithmetic and avoid using decimal variables and values. If necessary, review the integer remainder modulo operator, Mod, introduced in this chapter.

4 Future Value Calculation

You are planning to invest money and would like to know what your investment will be worth within a specified period. You have decided to develop a program that will allow entry of different amounts, different annual interest rates, and different number of years. This will aid you in determining how much you would like to invest. Design and develop a Console program that allows a user to enter an investment amount, interest rate in percent (i.e., 5.50 for a 5.5% interest rate), and a number of years. The program then should calculate and display the resulting maturity value at the end of the investment period. The formula for calculating the value for an investment that is compounded quarterly is

Maturity Value = Investment $\times$ (1 + Interest Rate / 4) $^{4 \times \text{Years}}$

Be sure to divide the interest rate entered by the user by 100 in order to convert the percentage value to a decimal value. An investment of $100,000 at 5.5% for 5 years should result in a maturity value of $131,406.65.

5 Slope and Intercept Calculation

Using the concepts presented in this chapter, design and write a program that accepts two sets of (X, Y) coordinates — (X1, Y1) and (X2, Y2) — and then calculates and displays the slope and Y intercept of the line that intersects the two coordinates. Use the Integer data type for the variables and input values. The calculation for the slope and Y intercept are as follows:

Slope = (Y2 – Y1) / (X2 – X1)
Y Intercept = Y1 – (Slope $\times$ X1)

For example, coordinates (2, 3) and (4, 5) result in a slope of 1 and a Y intercept of 1.

Decision Making

Objectives

You will have mastered the material in the chapter when you can:

- Code an If...Then...Else statement
- Code a nested If...Then...Else statement
- Code a Select Case statement
- Use logical operators in code

- Create compound conditions using parentheses
- Declare and use constants within code

Introduction

The program developed in Chapter 1 was coded to perform precisely the same computation for every set of data items that was processed. In some instances, however, you may not want a program to process each set of data items in exactly the same way. For example, a program designed to compute gross pay would have to use one formula to compute gross pay for employees who are paid on commission and another to compute gross pay for employees who are not. Therefore, the program must be coded to make a decision concerning which of two gross pay formulas to use.

In a program, **decision making** is the process of determining which of one or more code paths to take during the execution of the program. As you have learned, a procedure is a section of code that performs a specific task, such as a calculation. The sequential flow of control within a procedure, as illustrated by the flowchart in Figure 2-1 on the next page, is not sufficient to solve problems that involve decision making.

To develop an algorithm that supports decision making, the code must include a **control structure**, which is a portion of a program that allows a programmer to specify that code will be executed only if a condition is met. Figure 2-2a on the next page shows a type of control structure, called the **If...Then...Else structure**, which indicates that a program can take one or more actions, based on a certain condition. Figure 2-2a shows an If...Then...Else structure in which a condition is evaluated and its result either is true or false — only these two choices are allowed. The result — either true or false — sometimes is referred to as the truth value. If the result of the condition is true, then one action is performed; if the result is false, then a different action is performed. The action performed can be a single instruction or it can be another series of instructions. The If...Then...Else structure also is described in detail in Appendix A on page 111.

As shown in Figure 2-2a, a diamond-shaped symbol is used to represent a decision in a flow-chart. One flowline always will be shown entering the decision symbol, and two flowlines always will be shown leaving the decision symbol. A condition that must be evaluated either to true or false is

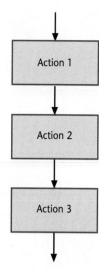

FIGURE 2-1

written within the decision symbol. For example, a condition might ask whether two variables are equal or whether the result of an expression is within a certain range. If the condition is true, one path is taken; if the condition is false, the other path is taken.

The **Select Case structure** is an extension of the If...Then...Else structure, in which more than two alternatives exist. Figure 2-2b shows a Select Case structure in which a condition is evaluated against four options and, depending on the result of the evaluation, one of four actions is taken. The Select Case structure also is described in Appendix A on page 112.

When writing code, the **If...Then...Else statement** is used to implement the If...Then...Else structure, and the **Select Case statement** is used to implement the Select Case structure.

After completing this chapter, you should be able to design a program using the If...Then...Else and Select Case structures. You also will learn how to code the structures using the If...Then...Else and Select Case statements. You will learn how to use logical operators in code and combine logical operators using parentheses. Finally, you will understand how to use constants in code.

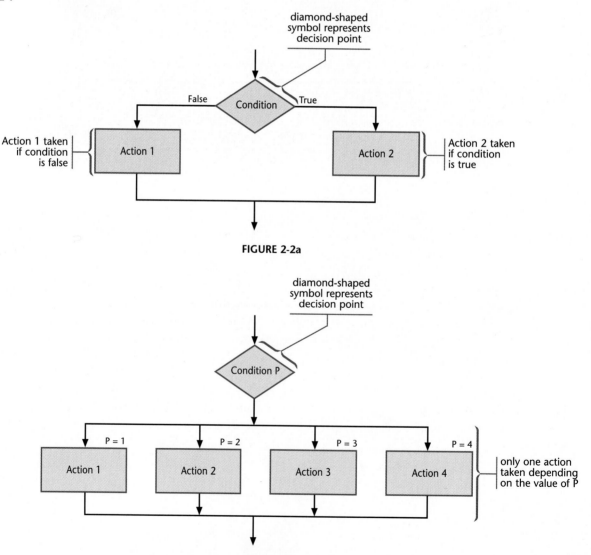

FIGURE 2-2a

FIGURE 2-2b

Adding Decision Making to the Commission Calculator Program

To illustrate the use of If…Then…Else statements in a program, this section shows how to develop a modified version of the Commission Calculator program from Chapter 1. The program includes two new requirements. First, a salesperson is eligible for a commission rate of 16% if his or her years of service with the company is greater than five years. Second, a salesperson is eligible for a 2% bonus on total sales if the salesperson's total sales are greater than $20,000 and total returns are less than $1,000.

The results of running the modified Commission Calculator program are shown in Figure 2-3. The program includes one additional input prompt for the salesperson's years of service.

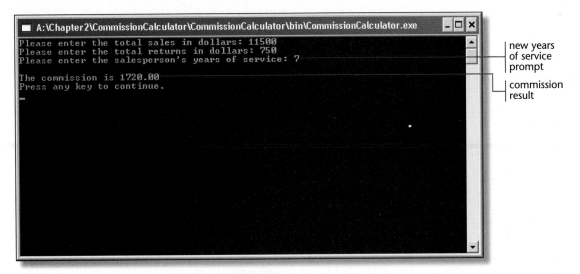

FIGURE 2-3

The program flowchart in Figure 2-4 on the next page illustrates the logic required for the modified Commission Calculator program. The flowchart shows two separate If…Then…Else structures. The first makes a decision based on the years of service and sets the commission rate depending on whether the years of service is greater than 5. The second is a nested If…Then…Else structure that first makes a decision whether total sales is greater than 20,000. If total sales is greater than 20,000, a second decision is made to determine if total returns is less than 1,000. If total returns is less than 1,000, the salesperson is eligible for a 2% bonus and the bonus is calculated.

Figure 2-5 on the next page shows the pseudocode for the modified Commission Calculator program based on the flowchart shown in Figure 2-4. Appendix A includes a more detailed discussion of pseudocode. The calculation of the commission uses a variable to store the commission rate, and the bonus is included in the calculation.

Figure 2-6 on the next page shows the code resulting from the design of the modified Commission Calculator program. The program is a modification of the Commission Calculator developed in Chapter 1. The modifications include the use of constants, additional variable declarations, an additional input value, the addition of two If…Then…Else statements, and a modification to the commission calculation. Each of these changes will be discussed in detail later in this chapter.

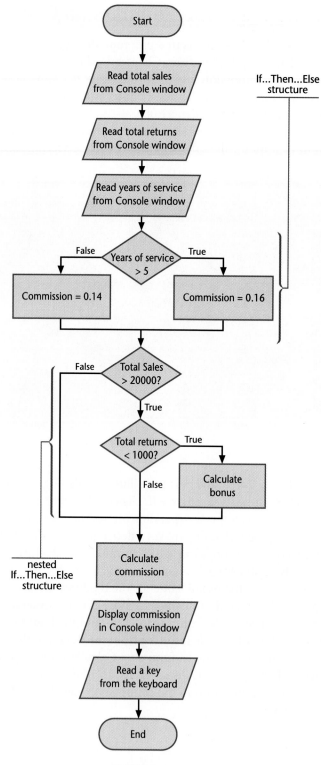

FIGURE 2-4

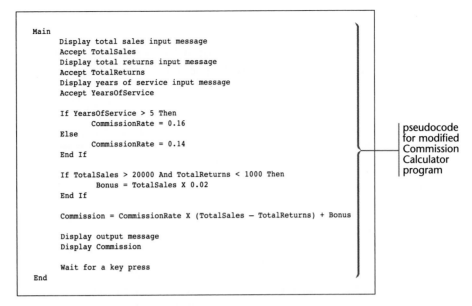

```
Main
        Display total sales input message
        Accept TotalSales
        Display total returns input message
        Accept TotalReturns
        Display years of service input message
        Accept YearsOfService

        If YearsOfService > 5 Then
                CommissionRate = 0.16
        Else
                CommissionRate = 0.14
        End If

        If TotalSales > 20000 And TotalReturns < 1000 Then
                Bonus = TotalSales X 0.02
        End If

        Commission = CommissionRate X (TotalSales – TotalReturns) + Bonus

        Display output message
        Display Commission

        Wait for a key press
End
```

pseudocode for modified Commission Calculator program

FIGURE 2-5

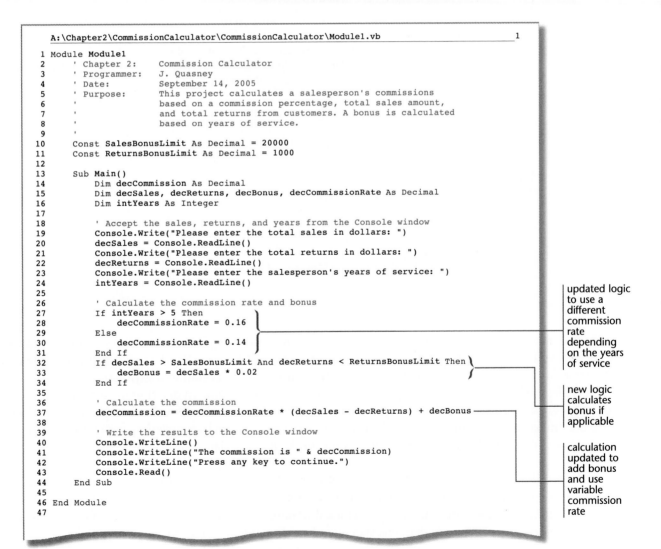

A:\Chapter2\CommissionCalculator\CommissionCalculator\Module1.vb   1

```
1  Module Module1
2     ' Chapter 2:      Commission Calculator
3     ' Programmer:     J. Quasney
4     ' Date:           September 14, 2005
5     ' Purpose:        This project calculates a salesperson's commissions
6     '                 based on a commission percentage, total sales amount,
7     '                 and total returns from customers. A bonus is calculated
8     '                 based on years of service.
9     '
10    Const SalesBonusLimit As Decimal = 20000
11    Const ReturnsBonusLimit As Decimal = 1000
12
13    Sub Main()
14       Dim decCommission As Decimal
15       Dim decSales, decReturns, decBonus, decCommissionRate As Decimal
16       Dim intYears As Integer
17
18       ' Accept the sales, returns, and years from the Console window
19       Console.Write("Please enter the total sales in dollars: ")
20       decSales = Console.ReadLine()
21       Console.Write("Please enter the total returns in dollars: ")
22       decReturns = Console.ReadLine()
23       Console.Write("Please enter the salesperson's years of service: ")
24       intYears = Console.ReadLine()
25
26       ' Calculate the commission rate and bonus
27       If intYears > 5 Then
28          decCommissionRate = 0.16
29       Else
30          decCommissionRate = 0.14
31       End If
32       If decSales > SalesBonusLimit And decReturns < ReturnsBonusLimit Then
33          decBonus = decSales * 0.02
34       End If
35
36       ' Calculate the commission
37       decCommission = decCommissionRate * (decSales - decReturns) + decBonus
38
39       ' Write the results to the Console window
40       Console.WriteLine()
41       Console.WriteLine("The commission is " & decCommission)
42       Console.WriteLine("Press any key to continue.")
43       Console.Read()
44    End Sub
45
46 End Module
47
```

updated logic to use a different commission rate depending on the years of service

new logic calculates bonus if applicable

calculation updated to add bonus and use variable commission rate

FIGURE 2-6

The If...Then...Else Statement

The function of the If...Then...Else statement is to perform decision making — that is, to allow a program to determine whether to execute one or more lines of code. The general form of the If...Then...Else statement is shown in Table 2-1.

Table 2-1 If...Then...Else Statement

General form:	1. If condition Then clause 1 Else clause 2
	2. If condition Then clause 1 clause 2
	Else
	clause 3
	End If
	3. If condition Then
	clause
	End If
	where condition is a relation that either is true or false and clause is a statement or series of statements. The Else keyword and subsequent clause are optional, as shown above in General form 3. General form 1 is called a single-line If...Then...Else statement; General forms 2 and 3 are called block If...Then...Else statements.
Purpose:	To indicate that a decision must be made, based on the evaluation of a condition. If the condition is true, Visual Basic .NET executes the clause after the Then keyword. If the condition is false and an Else clause is included, Visual Basic .NET executes the Else clause. After either clause is executed, control passes to the line of code following the If in a single-line If...Then...Else statement or following the corresponding End If in a block If...Then...Else statement.

Examples:	1. `If intAge > 21 Then`
	    `intCount = intCount + 1`
	`Else`
	    `intYoung = intYoung + 1`
	`End If`
	
	2. `If lngWeeklyPay >= 0 Then`
	    `blnPrintCheck = True`
	`Else`
	    `blnPrintCheck = False`
	`End If`
	3. `If strDegree = "M" Then`
	    `Console.WriteLine("Masters")`
	`End If`

As indicated in Table 2-1, the If...Then...Else statement is used to indicate that a decision must be made, based on the evaluation of a condition. The condition appears between the keywords, If and Then, and is made up of two expressions and a relational operator. A condition sometimes is called a **relational expression**, because the condition specifies a relationship between expressions that either is true or false. In determining whether the condition is true or false, Visual Basic .NET first determines the resulting value of each expression in the condition. Visual Basic .NET then makes a comparison between the two expression results based on a relational operator. An expression also can consist of a single variable, constant, or value of the Boolean data type. Table 2-2 lists the valid relational operators.

If the condition in an If...Then...Else statement is true, Visual Basic .NET acts upon the Then clause. A **single-line If...Then...Else statement**, as shown in General form 1 in Table 2-1, is used to perform a single task when the condition in the statement is true. A **block If...Then...Else statement**, as shown in General form 2 in Table 2-1, is used to execute more than one statement in response to a condition.

For a single-line or a block If...Then...Else statement, if the condition in the statement is true, all of the statements up to the Else clause are executed. If the condition is false, Visual Basic .NET ignores the Then clause and acts upon the Else clause. In either case, after executing the statements making up the clause, control passes to the statement following the If in the single-line If...Then...Else statement or to the statement following the corresponding End If in the block If...Then...Else statement. If no Else clause is present and the condition is false, then control passes immediately to the statement following the If or corresponding End If.

As you learned in Chapter 1, you can declare variables anywhere in code. If you declare a variable in a block statement, however, such as the block If...Then...Else statement, the variable is valid only inside that block statement. This is known as **block-level scoping.** The term, scope, is used to describe where a variable is valid within code.

Table 2-2 Relational Operators

RELATIONAL OPERATOR	MEANING
=	Is equal to
<	Is less than
>	Is greater than
<=	Is less than or equal to
>=	Is greater than or equal to
<>	Is not equal to

Coding If...Then...Else Structures

This section describes various forms of the If...Then...Else structure and the use of If...Then...Else statements to implement them in Visual Basic .NET code.

Simple If...Then...Else Structures

Consider the If...Then...Else structure shown in Figure 2-7 on the next page and the corresponding methods of implementing the logic in Visual Basic .NET. Assume that *strPaid* is a variable with the String data type representing whether an employee has been paid. If *strPaid* is equal to the value "Y", the person has been paid. If *strPaid* does not equal "Y", the employee has not been paid. The counters, *intPaidCnt* and *intNotPaidCnt*, are incremented as specified in the flowchart, to keep a count of whether employees have or have not been paid. **Counters** are variables that are used to keep a tally of how many times a specific activity occurs in code.

In the solution shown in Method 1 in Figure 2-7, an If...Then...Else statement resolves the logic indicated in the partial flowchart. The first line compares *strPaid* to the value "Y". If *strPaid* is equal to "Y", then *intPaidCnt* is incremented by 1 in the Then clause. If *strPaid* does not equal "Y", *intNotPaidCnt* is incremented by 1 in the Else clause. Regardless of the counter incremented, control passes to the statement following the End If.

Note that the first method could have been written as a single-line If...Then...Else statement without the End If. For readability purposes, however, it is recommended that you do not use the single-line If...Then...Else statement. Additionally, if more statements need to be added within the If...Then...Else statement, a single-line If...Then...Else would need to be rewritten as a block If...Then...Else statement.

Best Practices

For readability purposes, avoid the single-line If...Then...Else statement. Instead, use a block If...Then...Else statement and always code the statement with the End If keyword.

In Method 2, *strPaid* is compared to the value "Y" twice. In the first If...Then...Else statement, if *strPaid* is equal to Y, then the counter *intPaidCnt* is incremented by 1. In the second If...Then...Else statement, if *strPaid* does not equal Y, the counter *intNotPaidCnt* is incremented by 1.

Although both methods are valid and both satisfy the If...Then...Else structure, the first method is more efficient, as it involves fewer lines of code and thus requires less execution time. Therefore, Method 1 is recommended as a solution over Method 2.

Method 1: Using a single If statement

```
If strPaid = "Y" Then
    intPaidCnt = intPaidCnt + 1
Else
    intNotPaidCnt = intNotPaidCnt + 1
End If
```

Method 2: Using two separate If statements

```
If strPaid = "Y" Then
    intPaidCnt = intPaidCnt + 1
End If
If strPaid <> "Y" Then
    intNotPaidCnt = intNotPaidCnt + 1
End If
```

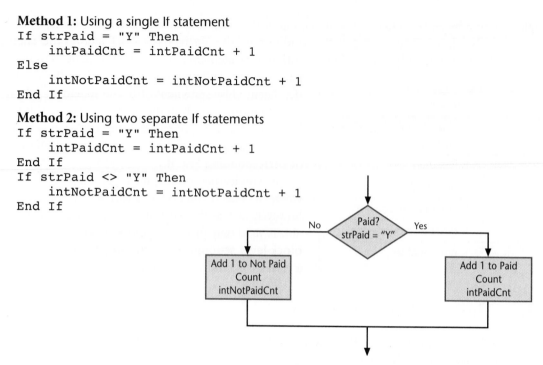

FIGURE 2-7

As shown in Figure 2-8 and Figures 2-9 and 2-10 on the next page, the If…Then…Else structure can take on a variety of appearances. In Figure 2-8, the code performs a task to perform only if the condition is true. Method 1, in which the If statement has no Else clause, is preferable to Method 2, which uses a null, or empty, Else clause, because it is more straightforward and involves fewer lines of code.

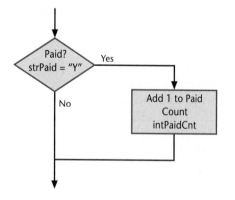

Method 1: Using an If statement with no Else clause

```
If strPaid = "Y" Then
    intPaidCnt = intPaidCnt + 1
End If
```

Method 2: Using an If statement with a null Else clause

```
If strPaid = "Y" Then
    intPaidCnt = intPaidCnt + 1
Else
End If
```

FIGURE 2-8

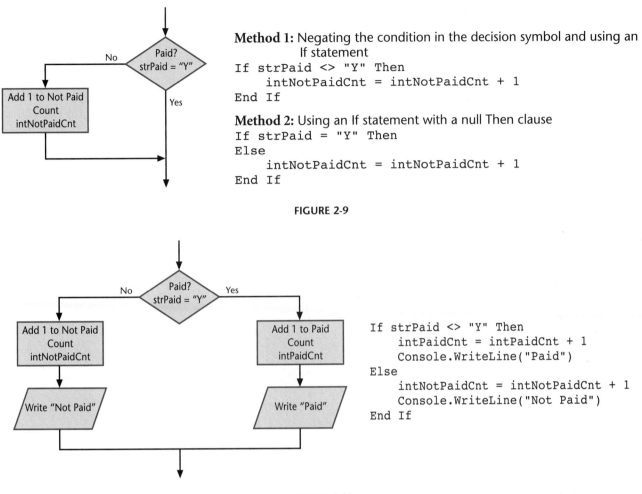

Method 1: Negating the condition in the decision symbol and using an If statement

```
If strPaid <> "Y" Then
     intNotPaidCnt = intNotPaidCnt + 1
End If
```

Method 2: Using an If statement with a null Then clause

```
If strPaid = "Y" Then
Else
     intNotPaidCnt = intNotPaidCnt + 1
End If
```

FIGURE 2-9

```
If strPaid <> "Y" Then
     intPaidCnt = intPaidCnt + 1
     Console.WriteLine("Paid")
Else
     intNotPaidCnt = intNotPaidCnt + 1
     Console.WriteLine("Not Paid")
End If
```

FIGURE 2-10

The If...Then...Else structure in Figure 2-9 illustrates how to increment the counter *intNotPaidCnt* when the condition is false. In Method 1, the relation in the condition *strPaid* = "Y" has been modified to read *strPaid* <> "Y" (that is, *strPaid* is not equal to the value Y). Negating the relation usually is preferred when the program must execute additional tasks as a result of the condition being false.

> **Best Practices**
>
> Negating a relation usually is preferred when a program must execute additional tasks as a result of the condition being false.

In Method 2, when the condition *strPaid* = "Y" is true, the null Then clause simply passes control to the statement following the End If. Either method is acceptable. Some programmers prefer always to include both a Then and an Else clause, even when one of them is null. Others prefer to negate the condition rather than include a null Then or Else clause.

In Figure 2-10, each task in the If...Then...Else structure is made up of multiple statements. If the condition *strPaid* = "Y" is true, the two statements in the Then clause are executed. If the condition is false, the two statements in the Else clause are executed. Although there are alternative methods for implementing the If...Then...Else structure, the method presented in Figure 2-10 is fairly straightforward and involves fewer lines of code.

The Nested If...Then...Else Structure

A **nested If...Then...Else structure** is one in which the action to be taken for the true or false case includes yet another If...Then...Else structure. The second If...Then...Else structure is considered to be nested, or layered, within the first.

Study the partial program that corresponds to the nested If...Then...Else structure shown in Figure 2-11. In the partial program, if the condition *strActive* = "Y" is true, control passes to the If clause that starts on line 2. If the condition is false, the Else clause on line 9 is executed. If control does pass to line 2, then a second If tests to determine if *strPaid* equals the value Y. If the condition on line 2 is true, lines 3 and 4 are executed. If the condition is false, then Visual Basic .NET executes lines 6 and 7.

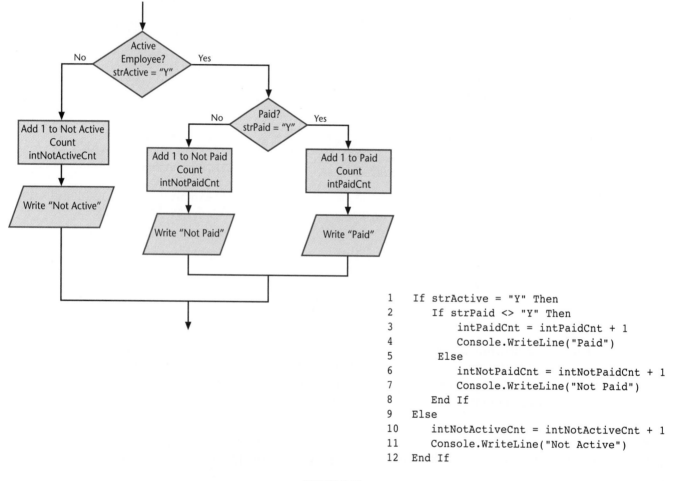

```
1    If strActive = "Y" Then
2       If strPaid <> "Y" Then
3          intPaidCnt = intPaidCnt + 1
4          Console.WriteLine("Paid")
5       Else
6          intNotPaidCnt = intNotPaidCnt + 1
7          Console.WriteLine("Not Paid")
8       End If
9    Else
10      intNotActiveCnt = intNotActiveCnt + 1
11      Console.WriteLine("Not Active")
12   End If
```

FIGURE 2-11

Visual Basic .NET requires that you end each If statement with a corresponding End If. Hence, the If on line 1 has a corresponding End If on line 12, and the If on line 2 has a corresponding End If on line 8.

In the partial program shown in Figure 2-11, note that only one of the three alternative tasks is executed for each set of data processed. Regardless of the path taken, control eventually passes to the statement immediately following the last End If on line 12. If...Then...Else structures can be nested to any depth, but readability decreases as nesting increases.

Best Practices

Avoid excessive nesting of If...Then...Else structures when possible, in order to improve readability of your code.

Logical Operators

In many instances, a decision to execute one alternative or another is based upon two or more conditions. In previous examples, each condition was tested in a separate decision statement. This section discusses combining conditions within one decision statement by using logical operators, such as And and Or. When two or more conditions are combined with these or other logical operators, the expression is called a **compound condition**. The section also discusses using the Not logical operator to write a condition that reverses a truth value.

The Not Logical Operator

The **Not logical operator** allows you to write a condition in which the truth value is **complemented**, or reversed. Recall that a condition made up of two expressions and a relational operator sometimes is called a relational expression. A relational expression that is preceded by the Not logical operator forms a condition that is false when the relational expression is true. Alternatively, if the relational expression is false, then the condition is true. Consider the following If statements:

Method 1: Using the Not logical operator

```
If Not X > Y Then
    Console.WriteLine("X is less than or equal to Y.")
End If
```

Method 2: Using other relations to complement

```
If X <= Y Then
    Console.WriteLine("X is less than or equal to Y.")
End If
```

Method 3: Using a null Then

```
If X > Y Then
Else
    Console.WriteLine("X is less than or equal to Y.")
End If
```

In all three of these If…Then…Else statements, if X is greater than Y, meaning the condition $X > Y$ is true, then the condition, Not $X > Y$, is false. If X is less than or equal to Y, meaning the relational expression is false, then the condition, Not $X > Y$, is true. All three methods are equivalent; however, Methods 1 and 2 are preferred over using a null, or empty, Then, as shown in Method 3.

To summarize, the Not logical operator requires the relational expression to be false for the condition to be true. If the relational expression is true, then the condition is false. Because the Not logical operator can increase the complexity of a decision statement significantly, you should use it sparingly.

Best Practices

Because the Not logical operator can increase the complexity of a decision statement significantly, use it sparingly.

The And Logical Operator

The **And logical operator** is used to combine two or more relational expressions in a condition. When two or more conditions are combined by the And logical operator, the expression is called a compound condition. The And logical operator requires both conditions to be true for the compound condition to be true.

Consider the following If statements:

Method 1: Using the And logical operator

```
If strEmpType = "FullTime" And intAge > 18 Then
    Console.WriteLine("Employee eligible for insurance.")
End If
```

Method 2: Using nested If statements

```
If strEmpType = "FullTime" Then
    If intAge > 18 Then
        Console.WriteLine("Employee eligible for insurance.")
    End If
End If
```

In both If…Then…Else statements, if *strEmpType* is equal to the value FullTime and *intAge* is greater than 18, then the message, Employee eligible for insurance, is displayed before control passes to the line following the End If. If one of the conditions is false, then the compound condition is false, and control passes to the line following the End If without the message being displayed. Although both methods are equivalent, Method 1 is more efficient, more compact, and more straightforward than Method 2.

Like a single condition, a compound condition only can be true or false. To determine the truth value of the compound condition, Visual Basic .NET must evaluate and assign a truth value to each individual condition. The truth value then is determined for the compound condition. For example, if *intI* is greater than 0 and *strC* equals "X", Visual Basic .NET evaluates the following compound condition using the And logical operator as shown:

```
If intI > 0 And strC = "X" Then Console.WriteLine("In stock")
```

    1. false   2. true

        3. false

Because one of the two conditions evaluates to false, the entire compound condition evaluates to false. An important characteristic of the And logical operator is that, even if the left side is sufficient to decide the condition, the right side always is evaluated. For example, if the left side of the And logical operator evaluates to False, the right side still is evaluated, even though the left side sufficiently decides the condition.

The Or Logical Operator

Like the And logical operator, the Or logical operator can combine two relational expressions to create a compound condition. The **Or logical operator** requires only one of two or more conditions to be true for the compound condition to be true. If all conditions are true, the compound condition also is true. Likewise, if all conditions are false, the compound condition is false.

Consider the If statements shown below, the first of which uses the Or logical operator:

Method 1: Using the Or logical operator

```
If decPay > 3000.0 Or decPay < 500.0 Then
    Console.WriteLine("Review employee pay.")
End If
```

Method 2: Using two If...Then...Else statements

```
If decPay > 3000.0 Then
    Console.WriteLine("Review employee pay.")
End If
If decPay < 500.0 Then
    Console.WriteLine("Review employee pay.")
End If
```

In Method 1, if *decPay* either is greater than 3000 or less than 500, the Then clause is executed. If both conditions are true, the Then clause also is executed. If both conditions are false, the Then clause is bypassed and control passes to the line following the End If.

Method 2 uses two If...Then...Else statements to resolve the same problem. Both methods are basically equivalent, with the exception that Method 2 writes the message twice if both conditions are true. Method 1, however, is more straightforward than Method 2. You also can write a single nested If...Then...Else statement without a logical operator that results in the same logic described in Methods 1 and 2.

As with the And logical operator, the truth values of the individual conditions are determined first, then the truth values for the conditions containing the Or logical operator are evaluated. For example, if *K* equals 4, *L* equals 4.9, *M* equals 4.8, and *N* equals 6.3, the following condition is true:

```
If K = 6 Or L = 2 Or M < N Then intCount = intCount + 1
     1. false     2. false     3. true
           4. false
              5. true
```

The Or logical operator requires only one of the conditions to be true for the compound condition to be true. In the previous example, one of the three conditions evaluates to true; the entire compound condition thus evaluates to true. If two or three conditions are true, the compound condition also is true. If all three conditions are false, the compound condition also is false.

Other Logical Operators

Additional logical operators, such as Xor, AndAlso, and OrElse also can be used in compound conditions. The **Xor logical operator** requires one of the two conditions to be true for the compound condition to be true. If both conditions are true, the compound condition is false. Likewise, if both conditions are false, the compound condition also is false.

As previously discussed, both the And and Or logical operators always evaluate both sides of a condition, even if the left side is sufficient to decide the condition. Two additional logical operators, the **AndAlso logical operator** and the **OrElse logical operator**, perform the And and Or operations, but include a feature called short-circuiting. If the left side of the AndAlso operator evaluates to False, the right side is not evaluated. If the left side of the OrElse operator evaluates to True, the right side is not evaluated.

Combining Logical Operators and the Rules of Precedence

As you have learned, logical operators such as And, Or, Xor, AndAlso, and OrElse, can be combined in a decision statement to form a compound condition. The formation of compound conditions that involve more than one type of logical operator can create problems, unless you fully understand the order in which Visual Basic .NET evaluates the entire condition. Consider the following If statement:

```
If X > Y Or T = D And H < 3 Or Not Y = R Then
     intCount = intCount + 1
End If
```

To understand how Visual Basic .NET evaluates this statement, you must know if it evaluates operators from left to right, right to left, or one type of operator before another.

The order in which a series of logical operators are evaluated is a part of what are called the **rules of precedence**. As discussed in Chapter 1, Visual Basic .NET has rules of precedence for arithmetic operations, called the order of operations. Visual Basic .NET also has rules of precedence for logical operators. Unless parentheses dictate otherwise, Visual Basic .NET reads from left to right and evaluates conditions using logical operators in this order:

1. Conditions containing arithmetic operators are evaluated first.
2. Conditions containing relational operators are evaluated second.
3. Conditions containing Not operators are evaluated third.
4. Conditions containing And and AndAlso operators are evaluated fourth.
5. Conditions containing Or and OrElse operators are evaluated fifth.
6. Conditions containing Xor operators are evaluated sixth.

Based on those rules of precedence, the compound condition in the previous If statement is evaluated as follows, assuming $D = 3$, $H = 3$, $R = 2$, $T = 5$, $X = 3$, and $Y = 2$:

```
X > Y   Or   T = D   And   H < 3   Or   Not Y = R
1. true      2. false      3. false      4. true
                  6. false            5. false
        7. true
                  8. true
```

Parentheses can be used to change the order in which conditions are evaluated when combining logical operators. As discussed in Chapter 1, in Visual Basic .NET, parentheses normally are used to avoid ambiguity and to group conditions with a desired logical operator. When parentheses are used in a compound condition, Visual Basic .NET evaluates that part of the compound condition within the parentheses first and then continues to evaluate the remaining compound condition according to the rules of precedence.

Using Constants in Code

As discussed in Chapter 1, when you want to use a constant in code, you first must declare the constant by telling Visual Basic .NET the name, data type, and value of the constant. To declare a constant, you use the **Const keyword**. Table 2-3 shows the general form of the constant declaration statement. Declaring a constant in code ensures that, if the value stated in the requirements changes in the future, you have to change the value in only one place in the code. Using a constant also makes the value's purpose more clear because the value is given a meaningful name.

Table 2-3 Constant Declaration Statement	
General form:	1. Const name As type = value 2. Const name = value
Purpose:	The constant declaration statement declares a constant that cannot change its value during the execution of code. The name of the constant can be used in code to represent the value assigned to the constant. The use of a constant allows you to change the value in only one place in the code in the future if the value stated in the requirements changes.
Examples:	1. `Const MaxVolume as Integer = 11` 2. `Const CurrencyString as String = "Dollars"` 3. `Const DrumCapacity = 1500.13`

Constants follow the same naming conventions as variables; these naming conventions are discussed in Chapter 1 on page 11. When naming constants, this book uses a naming convention that gives the constant a descriptive name but does not indicate the data type of the constant. When declaring a constant, the general form of the constant declaration statement indicates that a data type is not needed. Good coding practice, however, dictates that a constant or variable always be declared with a data type. Declaring a data type (1) makes the code more readable to others and (2) eliminates the time-consuming process of having Visual Basic .NET determine the data type during run time. Code is more efficient and foolproof if all constants and variables are defined explicitly with a data type.

> **Best Practices**
>
> A constant or variable always should be declared with a data type. Code is more efficient and fool-proof if all constants and variables are defined explicitly with a data type.

Coding the Commission Calculator Program

Figure 2-12 shows the modified comment header and constant declarations necessary for the modified Commission Calculator program. As shown in lines 10 and 11, two constants are declared for use in the code, rather than the numeric values, 20,000 and 1,000. The constant *SalesBonusLimit* reflects the current minimum amount of total sales that must be achieved before receiving a bonus. The constant *ReturnsBonusLimit* reflects the current maximum amount of total returns allowed before a bonus can be earned.

```
2      ' Chapter 2:    Commission Calculator
3      ' Programmer:   J. Quasney
4      ' Date:         September 14, 2005
5      ' Purpose:      This project calculates a salesperson's commissions
6      '               based on a commission percentage, total sales amount,
7      '               and total returns from customers. A bonus is calculated
8      '               based on years of service.
9      '
10     Const SalesBonusLimit As Decimal = 20000
11     Const ReturnsBonusLimit As Decimal = 1000
```

FIGURE 2-12

If you are coding the solution, you first must open the Commission Calculator program developed in Chapter 1 following the steps to open a project as discussed in Appendix B on page 128. Next, the comment header in the existing code should be deleted and the code in Figure 2-15 on page 45 should be entered after line 1 in the Commission Calculator program.

Coding an If...Then...Else Structure

The next step in updating the existing Commission Calculator program code is to declare three new variables for bonus, commission rate, and years of service (in addition to the existing variables for sales and returns). The code that accepts the years of service input from the user also must be coded.

Figure 2-13 on the next page shows the code that accomplishes these tasks. Line 15 is updated to include variable declarations for bonus and commission rate, and line 16 includes another new variable declaration for years of service. Lines 23 and 24 are new lines of code that accept the years of service value input by the user into the *intYears* variable. If you are entering the code in Figure 2-13, modify line 15 to declare two new variables and then enter the new code in lines 16, 23, and 24.

```
15          Dim decSales, decReturns, decBonus, decCommissionRate As Decimal
16          Dim intYears As Integer
17
18          ' Accept the sales, returns, and years from the Console window
19          Console.Write("Please enter the total sales in dollars: ")
20          decSales = Console.ReadLine()
21          Console.Write("Please enter the total returns in dollars: ")
22          decReturns = Console.ReadLine()
23          Console.Write("Please enter the salesperson's years of service: ")
24          intYears = Console.ReadLine()
```

FIGURE 2-13

Once the years of service is input, the years of service can be tested in an If…Then…Else statement to determine if the value is greater than 5. If the value is greater than 5, then the commission rate is 16%. Otherwise, the commission rate is the standard 14%. Figure 2-14 shows the If…Then…Else statement needed to make this decision. If you are entering the code in Figure 2-14, enter the new code in lines 26 through 31. When you enter the If keyword in line 27, Visual Basic .NET automatically adds the Then keyword in line 27 and the End If statement in line 31 of Figure 2-14.

```
26          ' Calculate the commission rate and bonus
27          If intYears > 5 Then
28              decCommissionRate = 0.16
29          Else
30              decCommissionRate = 0.14
31          End If
```

FIGURE 2-14

Coding with a Logical Operator

The second If…Then…Else structure shown in the flowchart in Figure 2-11 on page 38 shows a nested structure. This structure can be coded using the logical operator And to combine the decisions into one If…Then…Else statement. Line 32 in Figure 2-15 shows the use of the And logical operator to combine two conditions. If both conditions are met, a bonus is calculated for the salesperson, which is 2% of the total sales. By default, the *decBonus* variable is set to the value of 0 when it is declared. Therefore, if the salesperson is not eligible for a bonus, then the bonus already is set to 0. The *SalesBonusLimit* and *ReturnsBonusLimit* constants are used in place of the values of 20,000 and 1,000. Line 37 in Figure 2-15 shows the modified commission calculation. The variable *decCommissionRate* is used in place of the 0.14 value used in the Chapter 1 solution because the commission rate varies depending on the salesperson's years of service.

```
32          If decSales > SalesBonusLimit And decReturns < ReturnsBonusLimit Then
33              decBonus = decSales * 0.02
34          End If
35
36          ' Calculate the commission
37          decCommission = decCommissionRate * (decSales - decReturns) + decBonus
```

FIGURE 2-15

If you are entering the code in Figure 2-15, you should enter the new code in lines 32 through 37. After the code in Figure 2-15 is added to the modified Commission Calculator program, the coding for the program is complete.

Saving, Testing, and Documenting the Commission Calculator Program

After the coding of the modified Commission Calculator program is complete, the program should be saved and tested. The Save button on the Standard toolbar is used to save the program. After clicking the Start button on the Standard toolbar, the program executes. After entering total sales of 11,500, total returns of 750, and years of service of 7 as the inputs, the program displays the resulting commission of 1720.00, as shown in Figure 2-16.

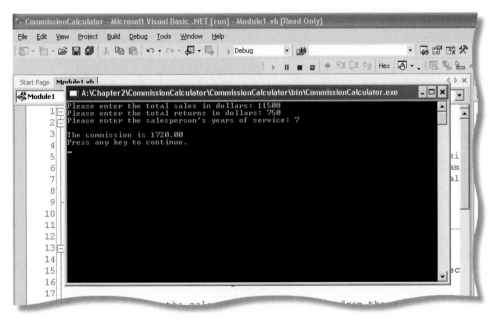

FIGURE 2-16

After saving and testing the code, a hard copy documentation of the program code should be printed for future reference, following the steps shown in Chapter 1 on page 20. Figure 2-17 on the next page shows the resulting printout of code.

```
  A:\Chapter2\CommissionCalculator\CommissionCalculator\Module1.vb                    1
 1 Module Module1
 2     ' Chapter 2:      Commission Calculator
 3     ' Programmer:     J. Quasney
 4     ' Date:           September 14, 2005
 5     ' Purpose:        This project calculates a salesperson's commissions
 6     '                 based on a commission percentage, total sales amount,
 7     '                 and total returns from customers. A bonus is calculated
 8     '                 based on years of service.
 9     '
10     Const SalesBonusLimit As Decimal = 20000
11     Const ReturnsBonusLimit As Decimal = 1000
12
13     Sub Main()
14         Dim decCommission As Decimal
15         Dim decSales, decReturns, decBonus, decCommissionRate As Decimal
16         Dim intYears As Integer
17
18         ' Accept the sales, returns, and years from the Console window
19         Console.Write("Please enter the total sales in dollars: ")
20         decSales = Console.ReadLine()
21         Console.Write("Please enter the total returns in dollars: ")
22         decReturns = Console.ReadLine()
23         Console.Write("Please enter the salesperson's years of service: ")
24         intYears = Console.ReadLine()
25
26         ' Calculate the commission rate and bonus
27         If intYears > 5 Then
28             decCommissionRate = 0.16
29         Else
30             decCommissionRate = 0.14
31         End If
32         If decSales > SalesBonusLimit And decReturns < ReturnsBonusLimit Then
33             decBonus = decSales * 0.02
34         End If
35
36         ' Calculate the commission
37         decCommission = decCommissionRate * (decSales - decReturns) + decBonus
38
39         ' Write the results to the Console window
40         Console.WriteLine()
41         Console.WriteLine("The commission is " & decCommission)
42         Console.WriteLine("Press any key to continue.")
43         Console.Read()
44     End Sub
45
46 End Module
47
```

FIGURE 2-17

The Select Case Statement

As previously discussed, the Select Case structure is an extension of the If…Then…Else structure in which more than two alternatives exist. The Select Case statement is used to implement the Select Case structure in code.

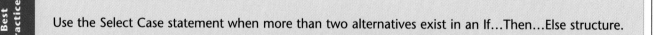

Best Practices

Use the Select Case statement when more than two alternatives exist in an If…Then…Else structure.

Table 2-4 shows the general form of a Select Case statement. As shown in Table 2-4, with a Select Case statement, you place the variable or expression you want to test after the keywords, Select Case. Next, you assign the group of truth values that make each alternative case true after the keyword, Case. Each case contains the range of statements to execute, and you can add as many cases as required. After the last case, the Select Case statement ends with an End Select.

Example 1 in Table 2-4 tests the variable *intSchooling* against the matchexpression, beginning with the first Case clause and continuing downward until a match is found. Only the range of statements that correspond to the first matched case in a Select Case are executed. For example, if *intSchooling* is equal to 0, a match occurs on the first case, and the string "High School" is assigned to the *strEducationLevel* variable. If *intSchooling* is 1, the value "Associates" is assigned to the *strEducationLevel* variable. If *intSchooling* is greater than 5, the value "Other" is assigned to the *strEducationLevel* variable. The keyword Is is required when a relational operator, such as < (less than), is used. If *intSchooling* is less than 0 and thus does not match any matchexpression, then the Case Else is executed, and the text "Invalid" is assigned to the *strEducationLevel* variable. Note that the Case Else clause is the last one in the list of cases. If a Case Else clause is included, it must be the last case.

In Example 2 of Table 2-4, the variable *strCode* is matched against several different categories of letters. The first case is executed if *strCode* is equal to the value A, B, or D. The commas in a list of expressions following the keyword Case are mandatory. If *strCode* is equal to the value C or the letters G through K, the second case is executed. The keyword To is required when specifying a range, such as "G" To "K". If *strCode* is equal to the values L through Z, the third case is executed. Finally, if *strCode* is equal to the value E or F, the last case is executed.

Note that this example contains no Case Else. The assumption here is that *strCode* is validated prior to the execution of the Select Case to verify that *strCode* always is equal to an uppercase letter between A and Z and that *strCode* contains no lowercase letters between A and Z. Hence, the Case Else is not required. If the rest of the code does not validate the expression, however, then you always should include a Case Else in the Select Case statement.

Table 2-4 Select Case Statement

General form:	Select Case testexpression 　　Case matchexpression 　　　　[statements] 　　　　　. 　　　　　. 　　　　　. 　　Case Else 　　　　[statements] End Select where testexpression is a string or numeric variable or expression that is matched with the matchexpression in the corresponding Case clauses; and matchexpression is a numeric or string expression or a range of numeric or string expressions of the following form: 1. expression, expression, . . . , expression 2. expression To expression 3. a relational expression where relation is <, >, >=, <=, =, or <>
Purpose:	The Select Case statement causes execution of the range of statements that follow the Case clause whose matchexpression matches the testexpression. If no match exists, the range of statements in the Case Else clause is executed. Following the execution of a range of statements, control passes to the statement following the End Select.

Examples:	```
	1. Select Case intSchooling
	       Case 0
	           strEducationLevel = "High School"
	       Case 1
	           strEducationLevel = "Associates"
	       Case 2
	           strEducationLevel = "Bachelors"
	``

continued on the next page

Table 2-4 Select Case Statement (continued)

```
                        Case 3
                            strEducationLevel = "Masters"
                        Case 4
                            strEducationLevel = "Doctorate"
                        Case 5
                            strEducationLevel = "Post-Doctorate"
                        Case Is > 5
                            strEducationLevel = "Other"
                        Case Else
                            strEducationLevel = "Invalid"
                    End Select
            2. Select Case strCode
                    Case "A", "B", "D"
                        dblInterest = .015
                        intTime = 24
                    Case "C", "G" To "K"
                        dblInterest = .014
                        intTime = 36
                    Case "L" To "Z"
                        dblInterest = .013
                        intTime = 48
                    Case "E", "F"
                        dblInterest = .012
                        intTime = 60
                End Select
```

Notes: If the Case Else clause is not included in a Select Case statement, as in Example 2, it is the programmer's responsibility to ensure the testexpression falls within the range of at least one matchexpression found in the accompanying Case clauses.

Table 2-5 shows several examples of valid expressions to use as match expressions in a Case structure. As indicated in Table 2-5, you can construct valid match expressions in several ways. In Example 1 in Table 2-5, the match expression is a list made up of the letters A to F, the letter M, and the value of the variable *strCode*. In Example 2, the match expression includes the variable, *decEmpSalary*, and the expression, *decMaxSalary* – 5000.0. As indicated earlier, if a relational operator is used, the keyword, Is, is required. The second value in the list of Example 2 shows that expressions with arithmetic operators are allowed. The third example includes a list of values separated by commas with the keywords, Is and To.

Table 2-5 Valid Match Expressions

EXAMPLE	MATCH EXPRESSION
1	Case "A" To "F", "M", strCode
2	Case Is = decEmpSalary, Is = decMaxSalary - 5000.0
3	Case Is < 10, 50 To 75, 90.7, Is > 1000

When specifying a range in the match expression of the Case clause, make sure the smaller value is listed first. For example, the range, Case 12 To –5, is invalid; the range should be stated, Case –5 To 12. The same applies to string values. For example, the range, Case "Nuts" To "Soup" is valid, but Case "Soup" To "Nuts" is not, because Nuts comes before Soup in an alphabetical list ascending from A to Z.

Chapter Summary

In this chapter, you learned how to implement the If…Then…Else structure using the If…Then…Else statement and how to implement the Select Case structure using the Select Case statement. You learned how to use logical operators in code. You also learned how to create compound conditions using parentheses. Finally, you learned how to declare and use constants in code.

Key Terms

And logical operator (39)
AndAlso logical operator (41)
block If…Then…Else
    statement (34)
block-level scoping (35)
complemented (39)
compound condition (39)
Const keyword (42)
control structure (29)

counters (35)
decision making (29)
If…Then…Else statement (30)
If…Then…Else structure (29)
nested If…Then…Else
    structure (38)
Not logical operator (39)
Or logical operator (40)
OrElse logical operator (41)

relational expression (34)
rules of precedence (42)
Select Case statement (30)
Select Case structure (30)
single-line If…Then…Else
    statement (34)
Xor logical operator (41)

Homework Assignments

Short Answer

1. Given the following:

   $X = 250$

   $Y = 450$

   $Z = 200$

   $E = 60$

   $F = 400$

Determine the truth value of the following compound conditions:

   a. `Y = 450 And E = 250`

   b. `X < 200 Or Z = 200`

   c. `E + F = Y - 500 Or Z = 0`

   d. `Y - E = 390 And Not (Z = 200)`

   e. `Y < 500 And F < 50 Or Z = 200`

   f. `Y < 600 And Not (F < 50 Or Z = 300)`

2. In each of the following compound conditions, indicate the order of evaluation by Visual Basic .NET.

   a. `intX > 0 Or intY > 0 And intZ > 0`

   b. `intX > 0 And intY > 0 Or Not intZ > 0`

   c. `Not intX > 0 And intY > 0 Xor intZ > 0`

3. Determine a value of *intCount* that will cause the condition in the If...Then...Else statements below to be true:

   a. If intCount * 3 >= 7 And intCount < 4 Then

          intCount = intCount + 1

     End If

   b. If intCount < 8 Or intCount = 43 Then

          decAverage = decSum / 10

     End If

   c. If intCount / 3 < 9 Then

          intCount = intCount + 1

     End If

   d. If intCount > 3 And Not (intCount = 3) Then

          Console.WriteLine("Employee is eligible.")

     End If

4. Construct code statements for each of the structures shown in Figure 2-18. Declare any variables you use and name the variables following the conventions used in this chapter.

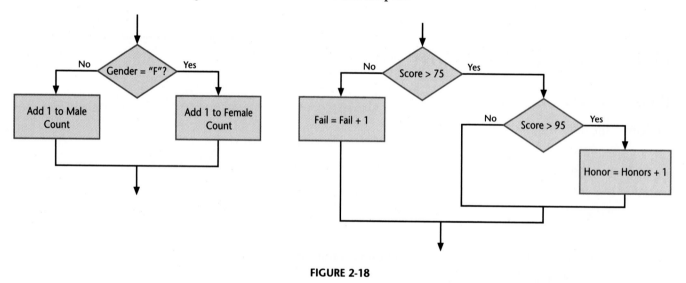

FIGURE 2-18

5. Assume *P* and *Q* are simple conditions. The following logical equivalences are known as DeMorgan's Laws:

     Not (*P* Or *Q*) is equivalent to Not *P* And Not *Q*

     Not (*P* And *Q*) is equivalent to Not *P* Or Not *Q*

For example, the logical equivalence

     Not ((*P* And *Q*) or (Not *P* And *Q*))

can be broken down to the following logical equivalent in two steps:

     Step 1 = Not (*P* And *Q*) And Not (Not *P* and *Q*)

     Step 2 = (Not *P* or Not *Q*) And (*P* or Not *Q*)

Use DeMorgan's Laws to write a logical equivalent for each of the following:

   a. Not *P* And Not *Q*

   b. Not (Not *P* And *Q*)

   c. Not ((*P* Or (Not *Q*))

   d. Not (Not *P* Or Not *Q*)

6. Construct code statements for each of the logic structures shown in Figure 2-19. Declare any variables you use and name the variables following the conventions used in this chapter.

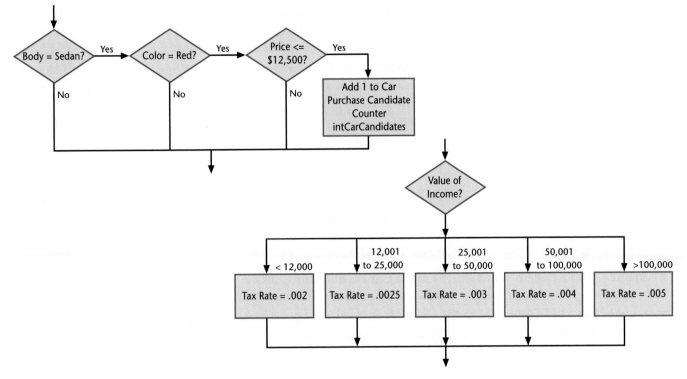

FIGURE 2-19

7. Given the conditions, $intA = 12$, $intB = 3$, $intC = 16$, $intX = 9$, and $intY = 2$, determine whether the message is displayed in the Console window for each of the following:

a. ```
If intA > 2 Then
        Console.WriteLine("The data is valid.")
   End If
```

b. ```
If intC = 15 Or intX > 3 Then
        If intB > 3 Then
             Console.WriteLine("The data is valid.")
        End If
   End If
```

c. ```
If intY = 2 And intX > 2 Then
        If intB <= 7 Then
             Console.WriteLine("The data is valid.")
        End If
   End If
```

d. ```
If intB + 1 < 5 Then
        If intC < intB * intY Then
             Console.WriteLine("The data is valid.")
        End If
   End If
```

8. Given five variables, *intQ*, *intR*, *intS*, *intT*, and *intU*, with previously defined values, write an If statement to increment the variable, *intTotal*, by 1 if all five variables have the exact average of 8. Use integer division when performing the calculation.

9. Given two positive-valued integer variables, *intFirst* and *intSecond*, write a sequence of statements to assign the variable with the larger value to *intLargest* and the variable with the smaller value to *intSmallest*. If *intFirst* and *intSecond* are equal, assign either to *intEqual*. Be sure to show variable declarations.

10. The values of three variables, *intFirst*, *intSecond*, and *intThird*, are positive and not equal to each other. Using If...Then...Else statements, determine which has the smallest value and assign this value to *intSmallest*. Be sure to show variable declarations.

11. Write a partial program to set *intFlag* = 0 if *intA* and *intB* are both 1, set *intFlag* = 1 if neither *intA* nor *intB* is 1, and set *intFlag* = 99 if either, but not both, *intA* or *intB* is 1.

Learn It Online

Instructions: To complete the Learn It Online exercises, start your browser, click the Address bar, and then enter the Web address `scsite.com/progvb/learn`. When the Programming Fundamentals Learn It Online page is displayed, follow the instructions in the exercises below. Each exercise has instructions for printing your results, either for your own records or for submission to your instructor.

1. **Chapter Reinforcement True/False, Multiple Choice, and Short Answer**   Below Chapter 2, click the Chapter Reinforcement link. Print the quiz by clicking Print on the File menu for each page. Answer each question.

2. **Practice Test**   Below Chapter 2, click the Practice Test link. Answer each question, enter your first and last name at the bottom of the page, and then click the Grade Test button. When the graded practice test is displayed on your screen, click Print on the File menu to print a hard copy. Continue to take practice tests until you score 80% or better.

3. **Crossword Puzzle Challenge**   Below Chapter 2, click the Crossword Puzzle Challenge link. Read the instructions, and then enter your first and last name. Click the SUBMIT button. Work the crossword puzzle. When you are finished, click the Submit button. When the crossword puzzle is redisplayed, click the Print Puzzle button to print a hard copy.

4. **Tips and Tricks**   Below Chapter 2, click the Tips and Tricks link. Click a topic that pertains to Chapter 2. Right-click the information and then click Print on the shortcut menu. Construct a brief example of what the information relates to in Visual Basic .NET to confirm you understand how to use the tip or trick.

5. **Newsgroups**   Below Chapter 2, click the Newsgroups link. Click a topic that pertains to Chapter 2. Print three comments.

6. **Expanding Your Horizons**   Below Chapter 2, click the Expanding Your Horizons link. Click a topic that pertains to Chapter 2. Print the information. Construct a brief example of what the information relates to in Visual Basic .NET to confirm you understand the contents of the article.

7. **Search Sleuth**   Below Chapter 2, click the Search Sleuth link. To search for a term that pertains to this project, select a term below the Chapter 2 title and then use the Google search engine at google.com (or any major search engine) to display and print two Web pages that present information on the term.

Programming Assignments

1 Simple If...Then...Else Statement

Draw a flowchart and then develop a program that calculates the fee due on a DVD rental after a customer returns the DVD. The normal rate is $2.50. A $1.00 late fee is added to the fee for every day after the two-day rental period, however. The user should be able to input the number of days that the DVD was rented. Be sure to use an If statement in your code to determine which charges to apply. For example, if the number of rental days is 5, then the rental fee is $5.50, as shown in Figure 2-20.

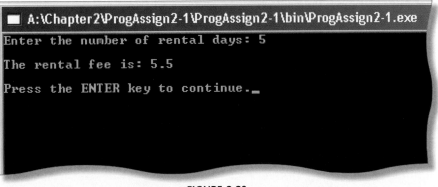

FIGURE 2-20

2 Stockbroker's Commission Calculator

Draw a flowchart and then develop a program that allows a user to enter a stock transaction and determine the stockbroker's commission. Each transaction includes the following data: the stock name, price per share, number of shares involved, and the stockbroker's name. Assume price per share = P. The stockbroker's commission is computed in the following manner: If P (price per share) is less than or equal to $35.00, the commission rate is $0.15 per share; if P is greater than $35.00, the commission rate is $0.22 per share. If the number of shares sold is less than 300, the commission is 1.25 times the rate per share. Display the results in a Console window, including the total commission earned. The displayed result should include the stock transaction data set and the commission paid the stockbroker in a grammatically correct set of sentences. Use constants to represent each of the values discussed above where applicable. For example, if the number of shares is 250, the price per share is 35, and the stock symbol is MSFT, then the result should appear as shown in Figure 2-21.

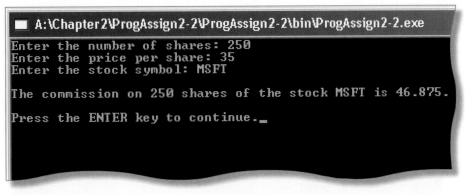

FIGURE 2-21

3 Select Case Statement

Design and develop a program that determines a mobile phone's usage charges based on the number of minutes used in a month. Use a Select Case statement to determine the late charge. The program should ask for the number of hours and minutes used in the month. For example, 130 minutes would be entered as 2 hours and 10 minutes. The usage charges are calculated as follows:

1. $15 if 150 or fewer minutes used
2. $28 if 300 or fewer minutes used
3. $32 if 350 or fewer minutes used
4. $36 if 400 or fewer minutes used
5. $.085 cents per minute if more than 400 minutes used

For example, if the number of hours is 5 and the number of minutes is 52, then the usage charges are $36.00, as shown in Figure 2-22.

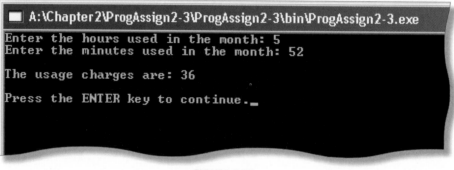

```
A:\Chapter2\ProgAssign2-3\ProgAssign2-3\bin\ProgAssign2-3.exe
Enter the hours used in the month: 5
Enter the minutes used in the month: 52

The usage charges are: 36

Press the ENTER key to continue._
```

FIGURE 2-22

4 Nested Select Case Statements

Design and develop a program that works as a paper, scissors, and rock game. Draw a flowchart and write pseudocode before coding the application. Allow each of the two players to enter their selection by typing 1 for paper, 2 for scissors, and 3 for rock. When the second player presses the ENTER key, a message displays the word that corresponds to their selection (e.g. Player 1 chose rock) followed by the winner. Use a Select Case statement based on the value of the first user's selection. Within each Case, use a nested Select Case statement based on the value of the second user's selection to determine the winner. For example, if Player 1 chooses paper and Player 2 chooses rock, then the winner is Player 1, as shown in Figure 2-23.

```
A:\Chapter2\ProgAssign2-4\ProgAssign2-4\bin\ProgAssign2-4.exe
Player 1: 1 for paper, 2 for scissors, 3 for rock: 1
Player 2: 1 for paper, 2 for scissors, 3 for rock: 3

Player 1 chose Paper
Player 2 chose Rock

The winner: Player 1

Press the ENTER key to continue._
```

FIGURE 2-23

Objectives

You will have mastered the material in this chapter when you can:

- Code a Do Until loop
- Code a Do While loop
- Declare and use arrays
- Manipulate strings of characters

- Use one-dimensional and multidimensional arrays in code
- Use arithmetic concatenation operators in code
- Code a For...Next loop

Introduction

The Commission Calculator programs developed in previous chapters were designed to operate in a linear manner, with the exception of the If...Then...Else structure that allowed the programmer to specify that one set of code statements should be executed if a condition was met, while another set of code statements should be executed if the condition was not met. A program also can be designed to repeat a set of code statements, based on whether or not a condition is met. For example, a program can be designed to accept input values repeatedly until the user has entered the maximum number of allowable input values. This process of repeating a set of instructions commonly is referred to as **looping** or **repetition**.

After completing this chapter, you should be able to code looping structures using the Do While, Do Until, and For...Next statements. You also will learn how to declare one-dimensional and multi-dimensional arrays to work with variables that store multiple values. Finally, you will learn how to work with strings of characters and how to use arithmetic concatenation operators in code.

Coding an Array and Loop in the Modified Commission Calculator Program

To illustrate the use of arrays and a loop, this section shows how to develop a modified version of the Commission Calculator program from Chapter 2. Rather than accepting user input from the Console window, data for several salespersons' monthly sales totals is stored in an array in the program. An **array** allows a programmer to represent many values of the same type with one variable name. The program then produces a report listing each salesperson's name, total sales, total returns, and commission on one line per salesperson. Finally, after processing each salesperson, the program writes totals for all of the sales to the Console window. The results of the modified Commission Calculator program are shown in Figure 3-1 on the next page.

Commission
Report
lists each
salesperson

report
totals

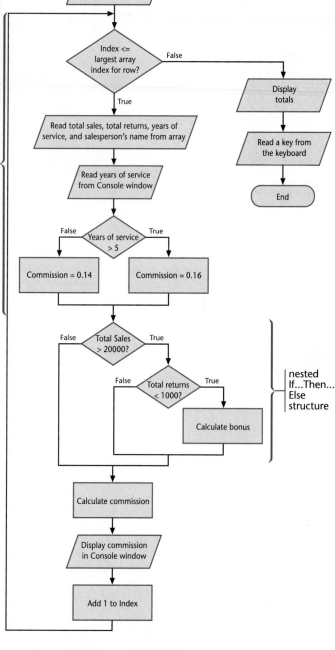

```
■ A:\Chapter3\CommissionCalculator\Commiss

          Commission Report

Name      Sales     Returns   Commission
----      -----     -------   ----------
Bradley   24861     2150      3179.54
Xu        19874     1050      3011.84
Ruiz      26197     2400      3331.58
Manes     23512     873       3639.70
Zach      18765     765       3350.24

Total sales: 113209
Salespersons: 5
Total commissions: 16512.90

Press the ENTER key to continue.
_
```

FIGURE 3-1

The program flowchart shown in Figure 3-2 illustrates the logic required for the new version of the Commission Calculator program. The flowchart shows a Do While structure that terminates after all of the salespersons' information has been read from the array and processed. The Index counter keeps track of which row of a two-dimensional array currently is being processed. The final process in the loop is to increment the Index counter by 1. After the loop terminates, the program displays totals, waits for the user to press a key, and then terminates.

Figure 3-3 shows the code resulting from the design of the modified Commission Calculator program. While the calculation of the commissions remains in the code on lines 42 through 53, the overall logic represented by the code is greatly changed. Modifications include the use of an array to store the salespersons' sales information (lines 14 through 18), the use of a loop to process each salesperson's sales information (lines 35 through 65), lack of user input from the Console window, and accumulation of totals (lines 59 through 62). Each of these changes will be discussed in detail in the following sections.

FIGURE 3-2

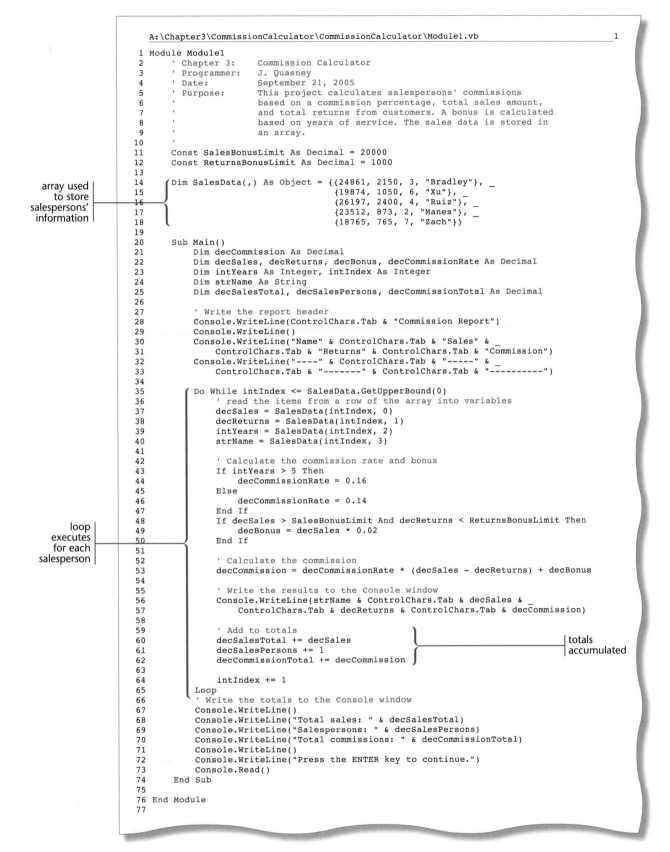

A:\Chapter3\CommissionCalculator\CommissionCalculator\Module1.vb   1

```vb
 1 Module Module1
 2     ' Chapter 3:      Commission Calculator
 3     ' Programmer:     J. Quasney
 4     ' Date:           September 21, 2005
 5     ' Purpose:        This project calculates salespersons' commissions
 6     '                 based on a commission percentage, total sales amount,
 7     '                 and total returns from customers. A bonus is calculated
 8     '                 based on years of service. The sales data is stored in
 9     '                 an array.
10     '
11     Const SalesBonusLimit As Decimal = 20000
12     Const ReturnsBonusLimit As Decimal = 1000
13
14     Dim SalesData(,) As Object = {{24861, 2150, 3, "Bradley"}, _
15                                   {19874, 1050, 6, "Xu"}, _
16                                   {26197, 2400, 4, "Ruiz"}, _
17                                   {23512, 873, 2, "Manes"}, _
18                                   {18765, 765, 7, "Zach"}}
19
20     Sub Main()
21         Dim decCommission As Decimal
22         Dim decSales, decReturns, decBonus, decCommissionRate As Decimal
23         Dim intYears As Integer, intIndex As Integer
24         Dim strName As String
25         Dim decSalesTotal, decSalesPersons, decCommissionTotal As Decimal
26
27         ' Write the report header
28         Console.WriteLine(ControlChars.Tab & "Commission Report")
29         Console.WriteLine()
30         Console.WriteLine("Name" & ControlChars.Tab & "Sales" & _
31             ControlChars.Tab & "Returns" & ControlChars.Tab & "Commission")
32         Console.WriteLine("----" & ControlChars.Tab & "-----" & _
33             ControlChars.Tab & "-------" & ControlChars.Tab & "----------")
34
35         Do While intIndex <= SalesData.GetUpperBound(0)
36             ' read the items from a row of the array into variables
37             decSales = SalesData(intIndex, 0)
38             decReturns = SalesData(intIndex, 1)
39             intYears = SalesData(intIndex, 2)
40             strName = SalesData(intIndex, 3)
41
42             ' Calculate the commission rate and bonus
43             If intYears > 5 Then
44                 decCommissionRate = 0.16
45             Else
46                 decCommissionRate = 0.14
47             End If
48             If decSales > SalesBonusLimit And decReturns < ReturnsBonusLimit Then
49                 decBonus = decSales * 0.02
50             End If
51
52             ' Calculate the commission
53             decCommission = decCommissionRate * (decSales - decReturns) + decBonus
54
55             ' Write the results to the Console window
56             Console.WriteLine(strName & ControlChars.Tab & decSales & _
57                 ControlChars.Tab & decReturns & ControlChars.Tab & decCommission)
58
59             ' Add to totals
60             decSalesTotal += decSales
61             decSalesPersons += 1
62             decCommissionTotal += decCommission
63
64             intIndex += 1
65         Loop
66         ' Write the totals to the Console window
67         Console.WriteLine()
68         Console.WriteLine("Total sales: " & decSalesTotal)
69         Console.WriteLine("Salespersons: " & decSalesPersons)
70         Console.WriteLine("Total commissions: " & decCommissionTotal)
71         Console.WriteLine()
72         Console.WriteLine("Press the ENTER key to continue.")
73         Console.Read()
74     End Sub
75
76 End Module
77
```

array used to store salespersons' information

loop executes for each salesperson

totals accumulated

FIGURE 3-3

Arrays

In Visual Basic .NET, an array often is used in conjunction with a loop, so you can create loops that deal efficiently with any number of values. As you have learned, an array allows a programmer to represent many values of the same type with one variable name. An array essentially is a set of variables, represented by a single variable. This variable, called an array variable, is used to store and reference values that have been grouped into an array. The variable name assigned to represent an array is called the **array name**.

Each variable, or element, stored in the array is identified by the array name and distinguished from one another by an **index** or **subscript**. In the array, the index is written inside a set of parentheses and is placed immediately to the right of the array name. For example, if the array name is *intBooks*, the first element in the array would be assigned the name, *intBooks(0)*. The first element of an array is assigned the index of 0 (zero), the second element of an array is assigned the index number of 1, and so on.

In many situations, using an array helps you write shorter and simpler code. Figure 3-4 illustrates the difference between using an array and using simple variables to store the same values.

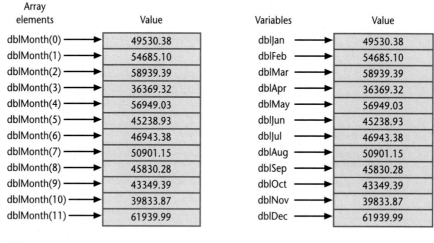

Array elements	Value		Variables	Value
dblMonth(0) →	49530.38		dblJan →	49530.38
dblMonth(1) →	54685.10		dblFeb →	54685.10
dblMonth(2) →	58939.39		dblMar →	58939.39
dblMonth(3) →	36369.32		dblApr →	36369.32
dblMonth(4) →	56949.03		dblMay →	56949.03
dblMonth(5) →	45238.93		dblJun →	45238.93
dblMonth(6) →	46943.38		dblJul →	46943.38
dblMonth(7) →	50901.15		dblAug →	50901.15
dblMonth(8) →	45830.28		dblSep →	45830.28
dblMonth(9) →	43349.39		dblOct →	43349.39
dblMonth(10) →	39833.87		dblNov →	39833.87
dblMonth(11) →	61939.99		dblDec →	61939.99

(a) Using an Array   (b) Using Simple Variables

FIGURE 3-4

The Dim Statement for Arrays

Before arrays can be used, the amount of memory to be reserved must be declared in the program using the Dim statement for arrays. The main function of the **Dim statement for arrays** is to declare to Visual Basic .NET the necessary information about the allocation of storage locations in memory for arrays used in a program.

Arrays created in Visual Basic .NET always have a **lower-bound value** of 0, meaning that is the value used to start addressing the elements in the array. The Dim statement for arrays also can declare the upper-bound value allowable for an index. The **upper-bound value** defines the highest value in the range of permissible values for the index of an element. If an array is to have five elements, you declare the array with an upper-bound value of 4. Such an array has indexes of 0, 1, 2, 3, and 4.

Table 3-1 shows the general form of the Dim statement for arrays. As shown in Table 3-1, an array can have one or more dimensions. The number of dimensions corresponds to the number of indexes used to identify an individual element. An array with only one dimension is considered to be a **one-dimensional array**. An array with more than one dimension is a **multidimensional array**, such as a two-dimensional or three-dimensional array. You can specify up to 32 dimensions, although more than three is extremely rare.

In Table 3-1, the Dim statement in Example 1 reserves storage for five Integer elements in the one-dimensional numeric array, *intSubtotals*. A one-dimensional array requires only one index per element. These elements — *intSubtotals(0)*, *intSubtotals(1)*, *intSubtotals(2)*, *intSubtotals(3)*, and *intSubtotals(4)* — can be used in a program in the same way that a simple variable can be used. For this Dim statement, the elements *intSubtotals(5)*, *intSubtotals(6)*, and *intSubtotals(-4)* are not valid, because the upper-bound value for indexes is set to 4, and the lower-bound value always begins at 0.

In Table 3-1, the Dim statement in Example 2 declares a one-dimensional array of Double values. No upper-bound value is specified, meaning that the array size is based on the number of elements assigned to the array in code. The elements are initialized in curly braces after an equal (=) sign. In the example, 5 elements are added to the array, meaning that the array's size is 5 and its upper-bound value is 4, because the first element has an index of 0. The element *dblLengths(4)*, for instance, is equal to the value of 5.0.

Table 3-1 Dim Statement for Arrays	
General form:	1. Dim arrayname(upperlimit) As datatype 2. Dim arrayname() As datatype = { initialvalue1, initialvalue2…} 3. Dim arrayname() As datatype where arrayname represents the array name and upperlimit represents the upper-bound value of the array. The upperlimit parameter can be repeated and separated by commas to define multidimensional arrays. Similarly, commas can be placed in the parentheses in form 2 to define additional dimensions. For all one-dimensional arrays, the number of elements in the array is equal to upperlimit + 1, because the first element of all one-dimensional arrays has an index of 0. If initial values are given, the array must not be given an upperlimit in the declaration.
Purpose:	The Dim statement for arrays declares array variables.
Examples:	1. `Dim intSubtotals(4) As Integer` 2. `Dim dblLengths() As Double = { 1.0, 2.0, 3.0, 4.0, 5.0 }` 3. `Dim shrCoordinates(99, 99) As Short` 4. `Dim intPoints( , ) As String = { { 1, 5} , { 4, 9} }` 5. `Dim intCounts() As Integer` 6. `Dim intValues (intUpperBound) As Integer`

Notes:	1. The lower-bound value of each dimension is 0.
	2. In Visual Basic .NET, the maximum number of dimensions is 32.
	3. If no upper-bound value is specified, as in Examples 2, 4, and 5 above, then the upper-bound value is set to the number of items to which you initialize the array (Example 3) or is set as you assign values to array elements.
	4. In the case of Example 4, a two-dimensional array is initialized, resulting in the following assignments:
	`intPoints(0, 0) = 1`
	`intPoints(0, 1) = 5`
	`intPoints(1, 0) = 4`
	`intPoints(1, 1) = 9`

The Dim statement in Example 3 declares a two-dimensional array with 100 rows and 100 columns. A simple way to understand a two-dimensional array is to think of it as a table with rows and columns. Each element in a two-dimensional array has two subscripts — for example, *shrCoordinates(2, 4)* — the first of which represents the row number and the second represents the column number. The total number of elements is the product of the sizes of the two dimensions. In this example, the Dim statement reserves storage locations for 100 × 100 or 10,000 elements for the array *shrCoordinates*.

Example 4 in Table 3-1 declares a two-dimensional array and initializes four elements. The element *intPoints*(0, 0) has an initial value of 1 and the element *intPoints*(1, 1) has an initial value of 9. Brackets are used to contain the initial values, and a second set of brackets separates each row of initial data. Example 5 declares an array of integers of unknown size and does not initialize any elements. Example 6 declares an array of integers of *intUpperBound* size, where *intUpperBound* is assigned a positive value greater than 0 prior to the Dim statement.

Declaring an Array in Code

Figure 3-5 shows the modified comment header and a two-dimensional array declaration that declares and initializes the array that stores the sales data. Lines 11 and 12 are unmodified from the Commission Calculator program developed in Chapter 2. Lines 14 through 18 include one line of Visual Basic .NET code separated by line-continuation characters. A **line-continuation character** indicates that the line of code continues on the next line and is used to increase the readability of code.

```
 2      ' Chapter 3:      Commission Calculator
 3      ' Programmer:     J. Quasney
 4      ' Date:           September 21, 2005
 5      ' Purpose:        This project calculates salespersons' commissions
 6      '                 based on a commission percentage, total sales amount,
 7      '                 and total returns from customers. A bonus is calculated
 8      '                 based on years of service. The sales data is stored in
 9      '                 an array.
10      '
11      Const SalesBonusLimit As Decimal = 20000
12      Const ReturnsBonusLimit As Decimal = 1000
13
14      Dim SalesData(,) As Object = {{24861, 2150, 3, "Bradley"}, _      ⎤ line
15                                    {19874, 1050, 6, "Xu"}, _           ⎥ continuation
16                                    {26197, 2400, 4, "Ruiz"}, _         ⎦ character
17                                    {23512, 873, 2, "Manes"}, _
18                                    {18765, 765, 7, "Zach"}}
```

FIGURE 3-5

The array declaration in lines 14 through 18 declares a two-dimensional array named *SalesData*. The elements of the array are of the data type Object. The Object data type is a general data type that can contain variables of different data types. Each element of the array, therefore, can be of a different data type. The array is initialized with five rows of data — one row for each salesperson — each containing four columns. The first column contains a salesperson's total sales. The second column contains a salesperson's total returns. The third column contains a salesperson's years of service, and the fourth column contains the salesperson's name. While the first three columns of the array represent integer values, the fourth column represents a string. For this reason, the array was declared with the Object data type.

If you are coding the solution, you first must open the Commission Calculator program developed in Chapter 2 following the steps to open a project as discussed in Appendix B on page 128. Next, the comment header in the existing code should be deleted and the code in lines 2 through 10 in Figure 3-5 should be entered after line 1 in the Commission Calculator program. Then, lines 14 through 18 in Figure 3-5 should be entered after the constant declarations.

Working with Strings

As shown in Figure 3-1 on page 56, the output of the modified Commission Calculator program is a formatted report. That is, a header is displayed, and rows and columns of data are aligned to produce an easy-to-read report. Visual Basic .NET provides a wealth of tools to format output so the output displays in a visually pleasing manner. One of these tools is a built-in set of constants that can be used to format output. For example, to use a TAB character to format output data, you use the ControlChars.Tab built-in constant. Another useful built-in constant is a carriage return character — ControlsChars.NewLine — which is used to start a new line of output.

Lines 28 through 33 in Figure 3-6 show the code needed to write the report header to the Console window. Four lines of report header information are written. The ControlChars.Tab constant is used to write TAB characters to the Console window in order to separate each column of output. For example, the Name and Sales column headings in line 30 are separated by a TAB character. Each individual string is joined using the string concatenation character (&). Lines 30 and 32 also include line-continuation characters, indicating that these lines of code are continued on lines 31 and 33, respectively.

Lines 23 through 25 also show several new variables declared for the modified Commission Calculator program. The *intYears* variable, which is used to store the salesperson's years of service, is included in line 23 of the code from the previous Commission Calculator program. The *intIndex* variable will be used to keep track of the current row of the array being processed. The *strName* variable will store the current salesperson's name. The *decSalesTotal*, *decSalesPersons*, and *decCommissionTotal* variables will be used to accumulate the totals for all of the salespersons' sales data. After all of the sales information in the array has been processed, the totals stored in these three variables will be displayed in the Console window.

writes report header | declares new variables required for modified program

```
23          Dim intYears As Integer, intIndex As Integer
24          Dim strName As String
25          Dim decSalesTotal, decSalesPersons, decCommissionTotal As Decimal
26
27          ' Write the report header
28          Console.WriteLine(ControlChars.Tab & "Commission Report")
29          Console.WriteLine()
30          Console.WriteLine("Name" & ControlChars.Tab & "Sales" & _
31              ControlChars.Tab & "Returns" & ControlChars.Tab & "Commission")
32          Console.WriteLine("----" & ControlChars.Tab & "-----" & _
33              ControlChars.Tab & "-------" & ControlChars.Tab & "----------")
```

FIGURE 3-6

If you are entering the code shown in Figure 3-6, you should place the insertion point at the end of line 23 and begin by coding the declaration for the *intIndex* variable. The *intYears* declaration already should exist on line 23.

Repetition and the Do Statement

As previously discussed, in programming, the process of repeating a set of instructions is known as looping, or repetition. Four basic types of loops or **Do...Loop structures** (Figure 3-7 on the next page) can be used in coding a program, two of which contain the decision to terminate the looping at the top of the control structure and two of which contain the decision to terminate the looping at the bottom of the control structure. A condition, which is either true or false, determines whether the code within the loop will execute again.

As shown in the code sample at the top of each of the four flowcharts in Figure 3-7, alternative forms of the **Do statement** can be used to implement the four types of control structures.

Implementing a Do While Structure

Do While condition
   [range of statements]
Loop

Repeat range of statements
while the condition is true.
Condition is tested before
the loop is executed.

(a)

Implementing a Do Until Structure

Do Until condition
   [range of statements]
Loop

Repeat range of statements
until the condition is true.
Condition is tested before
the loop is executed.

(b)

Do
   [range of statements]
Loop While condition

Repeat range of statements
while the condition is true.
Loop is executed before the
condition is tested.

(c)

Do
   [range of statements]
Loop Until condition

Repeat range of statements
until the condition is true.
Loop is executed before the
condition is tested.

(d)

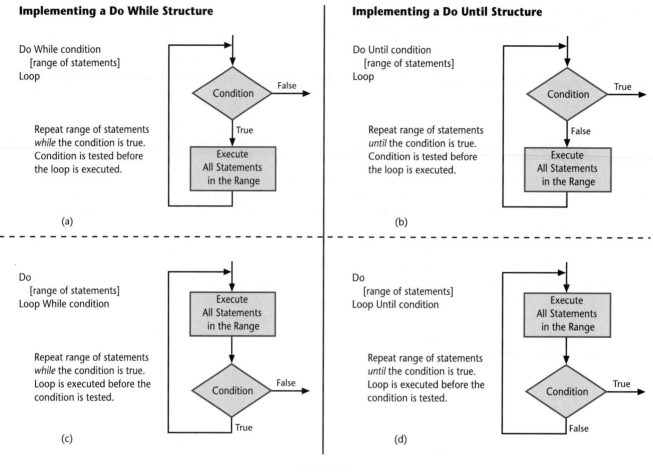

FIGURE 3-7

The conditions in each statement are created in the same manner in which conditions were created for the decision making statements shown in Chapter 2. Because the range of statements execute until a condition is met or while a condition is true, it is possible for the statements to execute infinitely in what is known as an **infinite loop**. When constructing a program, be sure to write code that will not result in an infinite loop occurring during execution of the code.

The Do While and Do Until Statements

A common form of the Do statement, called the **Do While statement**, is used to create a Do While structure (Figure 3-7a). A **Do While structure** repeatedly executes the series of statements in the loop as long as, or while, the condition is true. Another common form of the Do statement is the **Do Until statement**, which is used to create a Do Until structure (Figure 3-7b). A **Do Until structure** repeatedly executes a series of instructions until the condition is true. Both of these forms implement a loop where the decision to terminate is at the top of the loop. The Do While and Do Until statements also have forms that can be used to implement a loop when the decision to terminate is at the bottom of the loop (Figures 3-7c and 3-7d). As shown in Figure 3-7c, the Do Loop While statement executes a series of instructions before testing a condition; as long as, or while, the condition is true, the loop continues to execute. The Do Loop Until statement (Figure 3-7d) also executes a series of instructions before testing a condition; the loop continues to execute until the condition is true.

The general forms for the Do While and Do Until statements are shown in Tables 3-2 and 3-3.

Table 3-2 Do While Statement

General form:	1. Do While condition
	     statements
	  Loop
	2. Do
	     statements
	  Loop While condition

Purpose:	This loop causes the statements between the Do and Loop statements to be executed repeatedly. The loop is executed while the condition still is true. The first form tests the condition before looping, and the second form tests the condition after executing the statements within the loop once.

Examples:	1. `Do While intCount <= 20`
	     `intCount = intCount + 1`
	`Loop`
	2. `Do`
	     `intCount = intCount + 1`
	`Loop While intCount <= 20`

Table 3-3 Do Until Statement

General form:	1. Do Until condition
	     statements
	  Loop
	2. Do
	     statements
	  Loop Until condition

Purpose:	This loop causes the statements between the Do and Loop statements to be executed repeatedly. The loop is executed until the condition becomes true. The first form tests the condition before looping and the second form tests the condition after executing the statements within the loop once.

Examples:	1. `Do Until intCount > 20`
	     `intCount = intCount + 1`
	`Loop`
	2. `Do`
	     `intCount = intCount + 1`
	`Loop Until intCount > 20`

Selecting the Proper Do Statement for a Program

The flowchart for the program you are designing should indicate the type of Do statement to use in code. The type of Do statement you choose depends on the following three points:

1. If the decision to terminate is at the top of the loop, use Do While or Do Until (see Figures 3-7a and 3-7b). If the decision to terminate is at the bottom of the loop, use Do Loop While or Do Loop Until (see Figures 3-7c and 3-7d).
2. Use the While keyword if you want to continue execution of the loop while the condition is true. Use the Until keyword if you want to continue execution of the loop until the condition is true.

3. Select a Do Statement that does not include a negated relational operator. For example, to implement the Do While structure in Figure 3-8, you can write the following pseudocode:

```
Do Until Score = 99
or
Do While Score <> 99
```

Both of these statements generate the same result. The first statements indicate the loop should continue until *Score* is equal to 99. The second statement uses negation (that is, it uses an <> symbol to indicate is not equal to) to specify that the loop should continue while *Score* is not equal to 99. When implementing a Do While structure, it is recommended that you select the Do statement that does not include a negation, because it is easier to read.

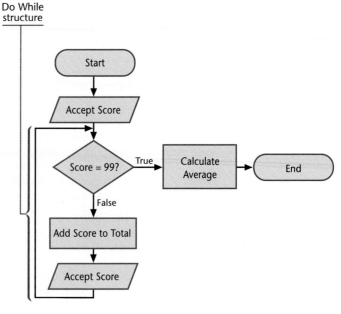

FIGURE 3-8

Best Practices

If the decision to terminate is at the top of the loop, use Do While or Do Until. If the decision to terminate is at the bottom of the loop, use Do Loop While or Do Loop Until. Use the While keyword if you want to continue execution of the loop while the condition is true. Use the Until keyword if you want to continue execution of the loop until the condition is true.

Best Practices

When implementing a Do While structure, always use the statement that does not require a negated relational operator, because it is easier to read.

Coding a Do While Statement

Lines 35 and 52 in Figure 3-9 show the statements necessary for the Do While loop that processes each salesperson's data. The statements within the loop execute while the *intIndex* variable is less than or equal to the upper-bound value of the first dimension of the *SalesData* array. The **GetUpperBound() method** returns the upper-bound value of a dimension of an array. The value 0 is passed to this method to indicate that the first dimension — the number of rows — is the desired dimension. The loop, therefore, executes while *intIndex* is less than or equal to 4, because the upper-bound value of the first dimension of the *SalesData* array is 4. The *SalesData* array contains 5 rows, as shown in Figure 3-5 on page 60. Recall that the index for arrays in Visual Basic .NET start at 0, so 5 rows results in an upper-bound value of 4.

Line 51 increments the *intIndex* variable after a salesperson's sales data has been processed. In the next section, the *intIndex* variable will be used as an index to indicate which row of the *SalesData* array currently is being processed. Incrementing the *intIndex* variable, therefore, has the effect of moving to the next row of sales data. This process continues until the *intIndex* variable exceeds the number of rows in the array.

```
35              Do While intIndex <= SalesData.GetUpperBound(0)          intIndex is compared to 4,
36                  ' Calculate the commission rate and bonus             the upper-bound value of
37                  If intYears > 5 Then                                   the first dimension of SalesData
38                      decCommissionRate = 0.16
39                  Else
40                      decCommissionRate = 0.14
41                  End If
42                  If decSales > SalesBonusLimit And decReturns < ReturnsBonusLimit Then
43                      decBonus = decSales * 0.02
44                  End If
45
46                  ' Calculate the commission
47                  decCommission = decCommissionRate * (decSales - decReturns) + decBonus
48
49                  ' Write the results to the Console window
50
51                  intIndex += 1                                         int Index is
52              Loop                                                      incremented by 1
```

FIGURE 3-9

If you are coding the modified Commission Calculator program, you first should delete the lines of code that prompt the user for input from the Console window (as shown in lines 18 through 24 in Figure 2-17 on page 46) . You also should delete the lines of code that display the results in the Console window (as shown in lines 39 through 41 in Figure 2-17). Then, lines 35, 51, and 52 should be entered as shown in Figure 3-9. Visual Basic .NET automatically will indent the lines of code in lines 36 through 51 after the Do While loop is coded.

Manipulating Two-Dimensional Arrays

Within the Do While loop, a salesperson's sales data is read and then displayed in the Console window. The current value of the *intIndex* variable determines which row of the array is being processed in each iteration of the Do While loop. As previously discussed, each row contains four pieces of data for each salesperson. The total sales for each salesperson is in the first column of each row. The sales for the first salesperson, therefore, are in the first row (row 0) and first column (column 0) of the array and can be expressed as *SalesData(0, 0)*. The name of the first salesperson is in the first row (row 0) and the fourth column (column 3) and can be expressed as *SalesData(0, 3)*.

Figure 3-10 shows the code that assigns the sales data for the current salesperson to individual variables. The current salesperson is indicated by the *intIndex* variable, which is incremented by 1 after the salesperson's data is processed and displayed. When the loop executes the first time, the *intIndex* variable is equal to 0. The first iteration of the loop, therefore, causes *decSales* to be assigned the value of 24861, *decReturns* to be assigned the value of 2150, *intYears* to be assigned the value of 3, and *strName* to be assigned the value of Bradley.

```
36                  ' read the items from a row of the array into variables
37                  decSales = SalesData(intIndex, 0)
38                  decReturns = SalesData(intIndex, 1)
39                  intYears = SalesData(intIndex, 2)
40                  strName = SalesData(intIndex, 3)
```

FIGURE 3-10

If you are coding the modified Commission Calculator program, the code shown in Figure 3-10 should be entered after the Do While statement in line 35.

Using Concatenation Operators

Chapter 1 introduced the string concatenation operator (&). Additional arithmetic concatenation operators also can be used as shortcuts to simplify assignment statements in which an expression modifies a variable. For example, the assignment statement

```
intTotal = intTotal + 1
```

can be written as

```
intTotal += 1
```

using the addition arithmetic concatenation operator, +=. The *intTotal* variable is assigned the original value of *intTotal* plus the expression 1. All of the standard arithmetic operators and the string concatenation operator have a concatenation operator that provides a shortcut when writing assignment statements. The use of concatenation operators makes code more readable. Table 3-4 lists the string concatenation operator, the arithmetic concatenation operators, and their meaning.

Table 3-4 Concatenation Operators for Assignment Statements

OPERATOR	EXAMPLE	MEANING
&= (string concatenation)	strFinalAnswer &= " is my final answer. "	strFinalAnswer = strFinalAnswer & "is my final answer."
*=	decX *=10.0	decX = decX * 10.0
+=	decX += 10.0	decX = decX + 10.0
/=	decX /= 10.0	decX = decX / 10.0
–=	decX –= 10.0	decX = decX – 10.0
\=	intX \= 10	intX = intX \ 10
^=	decX ^= 10.0	decX = decX ^ 10.0

Best Practices

Use the concatenation operators whenever possible in assignment statements to make code more readable.

Figure 3-11 shows the code that first writes a line of the report that contains the information for one salesperson, along with the calculated commission. This code executes within the Do While loop. Lines 60 through 62 use the addition concatenation operator to increment the report totals by the values for the current salesperson. As the loop iterates, the totals — *decSalesTotal*, *decSalesPersons*, and *decCommissionTotal* — are updated to include the current salesperson's information.

```
55          ' Write the results to the Console window
56          Console.WriteLine(strName & ControlChars.Tab & decSales & _
57              ControlChars.Tab & decReturns & ControlChars.Tab & decCommission)
58
59          ' Add to totals
60          decSalesTotal += decSales
61          decSalesPersons += 1
62          decCommissionTotal += decCommission
```

FIGURE 3-11

The final action that the Commission Calculator program must take is to print the accumulated report totals. Figure 3-12 shows the code that writes the totals to the Console window. This code executes after the Do While loop has finished processing all of the salespersons in the *SalesData* array.

```
66          ' Write the totals to the Console window
67          Console.WriteLine()
68          Console.WriteLine("Total sales: " & decSalesTotal)
69          Console.WriteLine("Salespersons: " & decSalesPersons)
70          Console.WriteLine("Total commissions: " & decCommissionTotal)
```

FIGURE 3-12

If you are coding the modified Commission Calculator program, the code shown in Figure 3-11 should be entered after line 54, within the Do While loop. The code shown in Figure 3-12 should be entered after the Loop statement. After the code in Figure 3-12 is added to the modified Commission Calculator program, the coding for the program is complete.

Saving, Testing, and Documenting the Commission Calculator Program

After the coding of the modified Commission Calculator program is complete, the program should be saved and tested. The Save button on the Standard toolbar is used to save the program. To test the program, click the Start button on the Standard toolbar to execute the program. As shown in Figure 3-13, after opening a Console window, the program displays the report header information, reads the array rows one at a time, performs the commission calculation on each row in the array, displays a line of output for each salesperson, and then displays the totals.

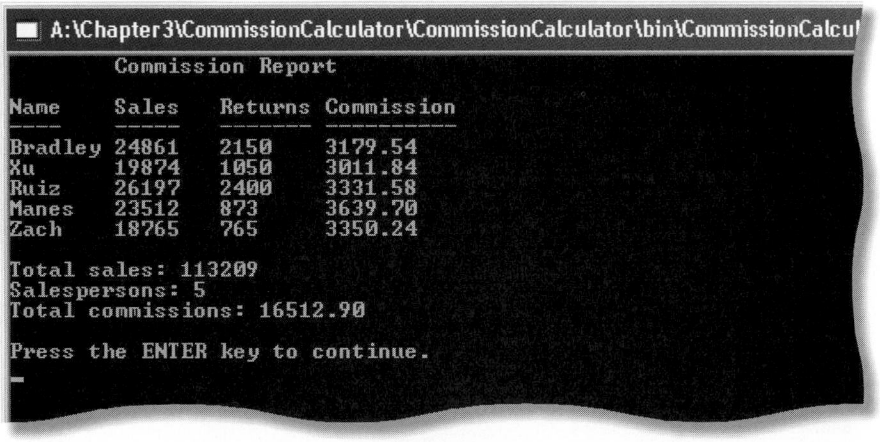

FIGURE 3-13

After saving and testing the code, the program should be documented. To print a hard copy of the program code, follow the steps shown in Chapter 1 on page 20. Figure 3-14 on the next page shows the resulting printout of code.

```
 1 Module Module1
 2     ' Chapter 3:      Commission Calculator
 3     ' Programmer:     J. Quasney
 4     ' Date:           September 21, 2005
 5     ' Purpose:        This project calculates salespersons' commissions
 6     '                 based on a commission percentage, total sales amount,
 7     '                 and total returns from customers. A bonus is calculated
 8     '                 based on years of service. The sales data is stored in
 9     '                 an array.
10     '
11     Const SalesBonusLimit As Decimal = 20000
12     Const ReturnsBonusLimit As Decimal = 1000
13
14     Dim SalesData(,) As Object = {{24861, 2150, 3, "Bradley"}, _
15                                   {19874, 1050, 6, "Xu"}, _
16                                   {26197, 2400, 4, "Ruiz"}, _
17                                   {23512, 873, 2, "Manes"}, _
18                                   {18765, 765, 7, "Zach"}}
19
20     Sub Main()
21         Dim decCommission As Decimal
22         Dim decSales, decReturns, decBonus, decCommissionRate As Decimal
23         Dim intYears As Integer, intIndex As Integer
24         Dim strName As String
25         Dim decSalesTotal, decSalesPersons, decCommissionTotal As Decimal
26
27         ' Write the report header
28         Console.WriteLine(ControlChars.Tab & "Commission Report")
29         Console.WriteLine()
30         Console.WriteLine("Name" & ControlChars.Tab & "Sales" & _
31             ControlChars.Tab & "Returns" & ControlChars.Tab & "Commission")
32         Console.WriteLine("----" & ControlChars.Tab & "-----" & _
33             ControlChars.Tab & "-------" & ControlChars.Tab & "----------")
34
35         Do While intIndex <= SalesData.GetUpperBound(0)
36             ' read the items from a row of the array into variables
37             decSales = SalesData(intIndex, 0)
38             decReturns = SalesData(intIndex, 1)
39             intYears = SalesData(intIndex, 2)
40             strName = SalesData(intIndex, 3)
41
42             ' Calculate the commission rate and bonus
43             If intYears > 5 Then
44                 decCommissionRate = 0.16
45             Else
46                 decCommissionRate = 0.14
47             End If
48             If decSales > SalesBonusLimit And decReturns < ReturnsBonusLimit Then
49                 decBonus = decSales * 0.02
50             End If
51
52             ' Calculate the commission
53             decCommission = decCommissionRate * (decSales - decReturns) + decBonus
54
55             ' Write the results to the Console window
56             Console.WriteLine(strName & ControlChars.Tab & decSales & _
57                 ControlChars.Tab & decReturns & ControlChars.Tab & decCommission)
58
59             ' Add to totals
60             decSalesTotal += decSales
61             decSalesPersons += 1
62             decCommissionTotal += decCommission
63
64             intIndex += 1
65         Loop
66         ' Write the totals to the Console window
67         Console.WriteLine()
68         Console.WriteLine("Total sales: " & decSalesTotal)
69         Console.WriteLine("Salespersons: " & decSalesPersons)
70         Console.WriteLine("Total commissions: " & decCommissionTotal)
71         Console.WriteLine()
72         Console.WriteLine("Press the ENTER key to continue.")
73         Console.Read()
74     End Sub
75
76 End Module
77
```

FIGURE 3-14

The For...Next Statement

The **For...Next statement** is another Visual Basic .NET looping statement, but it is different from the Do statements in that it has an automatic counter and condition built in. For this reason, the For...Next statement is ideal for counter-controlled loops. A **counter-controlled loop** requires that you initialize a variable prior to the loop, increment the variable within the loop, and then test the variable prior to looping again to see if the condition has been met. When you use a For...Next statement to establish a loop, it is called a **For...Next loop**.

> **Best Practices**
> When possible, use a For...Next statement as opposed to a Do While statement because it is easier to read, uses less memory, is more efficient, and executes faster.

The Execution of a For...Next Loop

Figure 3-15 shows a partial program that uses a For...Next statement to compute the sum of the integers from 1 to 100. The execution of the For...Next loop shown in Figure 3-15 involves the following steps:

```
1    ' Looping Using For…Next
2    intSum = 0
3    For intCount = 1 to 100 Step 1
4        intSum = intSum + intCount
5    Next intCount
6    Console.WriteLine("The sum is " & intSum)
```

Result
The Sum is 5050

FIGURE 3-15

1. After the comment line in line 1, line 2 initializes *intSum* to 0. When the For statement is executed for the first time, the For...Next loop becomes active, and *intCount* is set equal to 1.
2. *intCount* is compared with 100. Because it is less than or equal to 100, the statements in the For loop, in this case line 4, are executed.
3. When execution reaches the Next *intCount* statement in line 5, control returns to the For statement in line 3, where the value of *intCount* is incremented by 1, the value that follows the keyword, Step.
4. If the value of *intCount* is less than or equal to 100, execution of the For...Next loop continues.
5. When the value of *intCount* is greater than 100, control transfers to the statement (line 6) following the corresponding Next statement.

Table 3-5 shows the general form of the For…Next statement.

Table 3-5 For…Next Statement	

General form:	1. For *k* = initial value To limit value Step increment value
	    statements within For…Next loop
	Next *k*
	2. For *k* = initial value To limit value
	    statements within For…Next loop
	Next *k*
	3. For *k* As Integer = initial value to limit value
	    statements within For…Next loop
	Next *k*
	where *k* is a simple numeric variable called the loop variable, and the initial value, limit value, and increment value are numeric expressions.

Purpose:	The For…Next statement causes the statements between the For and Next statements to be executed repeatedly in a loop until the value of *k* exceeds the limit value. When *k* exceeds the limit value, control transfers to the line immediately following the corresponding Next statement. If the increment value is negative, the test is reversed. The value of *k* is decremented each time through the loop, and the loop is executed until *k* is less than the limit value.

Examples:	1. `For intItem = 1 To 20`
	   `Next intItem`
	2. `For intAmount = -5 To 15 Step 2`
	   `Next`
	3. `For intCount = 10 To -5 Step -3`
	   `Next`
	4. `For intTax = 0 To 10 Step 0.1`
	   `Next intTax`
	5. `For intTotal = intStart To intFinish Step intIncrement`
	   `Next`
	6. `For S = A + 5 To C / D Step F * B`
	   `Next`
	7. `For I = 20 To 20`
	   `Next I`
	8. `For J = 20 To 1 Step -1`
	   `Next J`
	9. `For intItem As Integer = 1 To 20`
	   `Next intItem`

Note:	If the keyword Step is not used, then the increment value defaults to 1.

As shown in Figure 3-16, the **range** of a For…Next loop is the set of statements beginning with the For statement and continuing up to and including the Next statement that has the same loop variable.

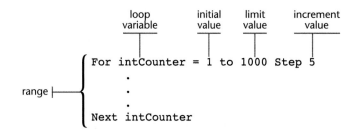

FIGURE 3-16

Table 3-6 summarizes several program tasks that can be completed using the For...Next loop.

Table 3-6 Using the For...Next Statement

TASK	REMARKS

Stepping by 1	Many applications call for incrementing, or stepping, the loop variable by 1 each time the For executed. You can write such a For statement as follows:
	`For Rate = 1 To 12 Step 1`
	or
	`For Rate = 1 To 12`

Stepping by a value other than 1	Some applications call for the loop variable to be incremented by a value other than 1. You can write such a For statement as follows: `For Rate = 1 To 12 Step 3` to step through the *Rate* values of 1, 4, 7, 10, and 13. The loop terminates when the loop variable *Rate* becomes 13 because this is greater than the value of the limit, which is 12.

Initializing the loop variable to a value other than 1	You can write such a For statement as follows:
	`For Rate = 8 To 16 Step 2`
	to intialize the loop variable to a value other than 1. Some applications call for initializing the loop variable to zero or some negative value. For example, the statements
	`For Temp = 0 To 10`
	or
	`For Temp = -6 To 12`
	both are valid. It is not necessary to initialize the loop variable to 1.

Decimal fraction values in a For statement	The values in a For statement can be decimal fraction numbers. You can write such a For statement as follows: `For Rate = 11.5 To 12.5 Step .1` This For statement loops between the values 11.5 and 12.5, inclusive, in increments of .1.
Negative values in a For statement	The step value in a For statement can be negative. You can write such a For statement as follows: `For Rate = 8 To 0 Step -1` This statement loops and the *Rate* variable is decremented from 8 to 0. The negative step value in the For statement causes the test to be reversed, and the loop variable is decremented until it is less than the limit value.
Variables in a For statement	The values in a For statement can be variables as well as numeric constants. You can write such a For statement as follows: `For Rate = Rate1 To Rate2 Step Increment`
Using expressions as values in a For statement	The values in a For statement can be complex numeric expressions. You can write such a For statement as follows: `For Y = X / Z To A * B Step V ^ 2`
Redefining For...Next loop values	After the For statement is executed, the initial, limit, and increment values are set and cannot be modified or changed while the For loop is active. Visual Basic .NET simply disregards any attempt to redefine them.
Iterations in a For loop	The number of **iterations**, or repetitions, specified by a For statement can be computed using the following formula: $$\text{Number of Iterations} = \frac{\text{LimitValue} - \text{InitialValue}}{\text{IncrementValue}} + 1$$ where the ratio is performed in integer arithmetic so that the quotient is truncated to the next lowest integer. For example, `For intTemp = -2 To 30 Step 2` Using the formula, the number of iterations is $\dfrac{30 - (-2)}{2} + 1 = 16 + 1 = 17$

Exiting a Loop Prematurely — The Exit Statement

Certain looping situations require a premature exit from the loop. Visual Basic .NET includes the **Exit statement** for terminating any loop early. Although the Exit statement can be used to exit any loop, the Exit statement typically is reserved for use when an error condition or unusual circumstances occur in the statements in the loop.

The general form of the Exit statement is given in Table 3-7.

Table 3-7 Exit Statement	
General form:	1. Exit statement where statement is For or Do.
Purpose:	The Exit statement allows for the premature exit of a For...Next or Do loop.
Examples:	1. `Exit For` 2. `Exit Do`

> **Best Practices**
>
> Use the Exit statement sparingly in order to keep the logic of code more readable. Typically, the use of the Exit statement is reserved for use when an error condition or unusual circumstance occurs within a loop.

Chapter Summary

In this chapter, you learned how to code looping structures, including the Do While, Do Until, and For...Next statements. You also learned how to declare and use one-dimensional and multi-dimensional arrays in code. You learned how to concatenate and work with strings in code. Finally, you learned how to work with arithmetic concatenation operators.

Key Terms

array (55)
array name (58)
array variable (58)
counter-controlled loop (69)
Dim statement for arrays (58)
Do statement (61)
Do...Loop structures (61)
Do Until statement (62)
Do Until structure (62)

Do While statement (62)
Do While structure (62)
Exit statement (72)
For...Next loop (69)
For...Next statement (69)
GetUpperBound() method (64)
index (58)
infinite loop (62)
iterations (71)

line-continuation character (60)
looping (55)
lower-bound value (58)
multidimensional array (58)
one-dimensional array (58)
range (70)
repetition (55)
subscript (58)
upper-bound value (58)

Homework Assignments

Short Answer

1. Identify the error(s), if any, in each of the following:

   a. `Dim intInventory As Integer = {1, 3, 5, 7}`

   b. `Dim strErrors(2) As String = {"Bad phone number", "Bad ZIP", "Missing name"}`

   c. `Dim intX(,) As Integer = {4, 3, 4, 3}`

   d. `Dim intX() As Integer = {4, 3, "Jones"}`

2. Given the two two-dimensional arrays *intArray1* and *intArray2*, each of which has 10 rows and 10 columns and is of the Integer data type, write a partial program using a For loop to compute the sum (*intTotal*) of all of the elements of the two arrays efficiently that have equal index values for row and column. That is, find the following:

   $intTotal = intArray1(0, 0) + intArray1(1, 1) + \ldots + intArray1(20, 20) + intArray2(0, 0) + intArray2(1, 1) + \ldots$ $intArray2(10, 10)$

3. Given the following partial program, what displays in the Console window when the code is executed?

```
intX = 1
For intOuter = 1 To 5
    intY = 0
    intX += 2
    For intInner = 1 To 2
        intY += intX + 2
        Console.WriteLine(intX & " " & intY)
    Next intInner
Next intOuter
```

4. Given the following partial program, how many times do the statements in the loop execute?

```
intCount = 7
intCount *= 3
Do While (intCount > 14 And intCount < 97)
    intCount +=3
Loop
```

5. Identify the syntax and logic error(s), if any, in each of the following For statements:

   a. `For intIndex = 10 To -10`

   b. `For intIndex = -10 To 10 Step -1`

   c. `For intCount = intX To intY Step -intY`

   d. `Dim intCount as String`
   `   For intCount = 0 To 7`

   e. `For intValue As Integer = 9 To 0`

6. How many lines will be displayed in the Console window in the following code segment?

```
For intX = 1 To 12
    For intY = 1 To 3
        For intZ = 1 To 7
            Console.WriteLine(intZ)
        Next intZ
    Next intY
Next intX
```

7. Consider the following types of Do and For...Next statements.

    a. Do While...Loop   b. Do Until...Loop

    c. Do...Loop While   d. Do...Loop Until

    e. For...Next

    Answer the following questions for each type of looping statement.

    (1) Is the test made before or after the range of statements is executed?

    (2) What is the minimum number of times the range of statements is executed?

    (3) Does the loop terminate when the condition is true or false?

8. For each set below, write a Do statement and then a For statement. With the Do statement, include the statements required to initialize and increment Initial.

Set	Initial	Limit	Increment
1	1	34	3
2	5	50	5
3	-10	0	2
4	50	100	2
5	2	13	.5

9. Given the array *intArray* has four rows and four columns and that the elements of the array *intArray* are assigned the following values:

3	6	2	8
5	7	3	0
3	5	7	9
2	4	8	6

What will be the final arrangement of the array *intArray* after each of the following partial programs executes?

a.

```
For intI = 0 To 3
    For intJ = 0 To 3
        intArray (intI, intJ) = intArray (intI, intJ)
    Next intJ
Next intI
```

b.
```
intJ = 1
For intI = 0 To 3
    intArray (intI, intJ) = intArray (intI, intJ + 1)
Next intI
```
c.
```
For intI = 0 To 3
    intArray(intI, 2) = intArray (intI, 1)
Next intI
```

10. Rewrite the following as valid assignment statements without using concatenation operators.
   a. `intValue *= 22`   b. `dblVal /= 20`
   c. `decTotal +=10.0`   d. `dblSquare ^= 2`

Learn It Online

Instructions: To complete the Learn It Online exercises, start your browser, click the Address bar, and then enter the Web address `scsite.com/progvb/learn`. When the Programming Fundamentals Learn It Online page is displayed, follow the instructions in the exercises below. Each exercise has instructions for printing your results, either for your own records or for submission to your instructor.

1. **Chapter Reinforcement True/False, Multiple Choice, and Short Answer**   Below Chapter 3, click the Chapter Reinforcement link. Print the quiz by clicking Print on the File menu for each page. Answer each question.

2. **Practice Test**   Below Chapter 3, click the Practice Test link. Answer each question, enter your first and last name at the bottom of the page, and then click the Grade Test button. When the graded practice test is displayed on your screen, click Print on the File menu to print a hard copy. Continue to take practice tests until you score 80% or better.

3. **Crossword Puzzle Challenge**   Below Chapter 3, click the Crossword Puzzle Challenge link. Read the instructions, and then enter your first and last name. Click the SUBMIT button. Work the crossword puzzle. When you are finished, click the Submit button. When the crossword puzzle is redisplayed, click the Print Puzzle button to print a hard copy.

4. **Tips and Tricks**   Below Chapter 3, click the Tips and Tricks link. Click a topic that pertains to Chapter 3. Right-click the information and then click Print on the shortcut menu. Construct a brief example of what the information relates to in Visual Basic .NET to confirm you understand how to use the tip or trick.

5. **Newsgroups**   Below Chapter 3, click the Newsgroups link. Click a topic that pertains to Chapter 3. Print three comments.

6. **Expanding Your Horizons**   Below Chapter 3, click the Expanding Your Horizons link. Click a topic that pertains to Chapter 3. Print the information. Construct a brief example of what the information relates to in Visual Basic .NET to confirm you understand the contents of the article.

7. **Search Sleuth**   Below Chapter 3, click the Search Sleuth link. To search for a term that pertains to this chapter, select a term below the Chapter 3 title and then use the Google search engine at google.com (or any major search engine) to display and print two Web pages that present information on the term.

Programming Assignments

1 Computing a Factorial

A factorial can be used to determine the number of ways that n objects can be combined, or permuted. The symbol $n!$ is used to represent a factorial, which is the product of the first n positive integers. For example, 5 factorial or $5! = 5 * 4 * 3 * 2 * 1$. The general equation is:

$$n! = n * (n - 1) * (n - 2) * \ldots * 1$$

A factorial uses recursive definition, in which the result of the first operation is returned to the original function and used in the second operation, the result of the second operation is returned to the function and used in the third operation, and so on.

Construct a program that will accept a positive integer from the Console window and then compute its factorial. For example, an input value of 5 should result in a factorial result of 120, as shown in Figure 3-17. The recursive definition used in the program is as follows:

If $n = 1$, then $n = 1$, otherwise $n! = n * (n - 1)!$

FIGURE 3-17

2 Telephone Number Lookup

Design and develop a program that requests a person's last name and then displays the person's telephone number. Use a two-dimensional array to store names and telephone numbers given the values in the table below:

NAME	TELEPHONE NUMBER
Selle	555-9389
Furino	555-3990
Binaku	555-4000
Wathier	555-1925
Soder	555-6843

Accept a name from the Console window and then use a Do Until statement to find the name in the array. Display a user-friendly message along with the telephone number in the Console window. Display an error message if the name is not found. Be careful not to cause an infinite loop if the name is not found. For example, entering a name of Wathier should result in a phone number of 555-1925, as shown in Figure 3-18.

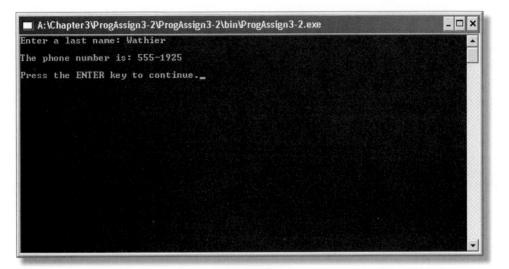

FIGURE 3-18

3 Using a Sentinel Value to Terminate a Loop

Design and develop a program that accepts test score values from the Console window until the user enters the value –1. The value –1 is called a sentinel value, which is used to tell the loop to exit when the number of iterations is not known in advance. Use an appropriate looping structure based on a flowchart that you develop for the program. Keep a running total of the values entered by the user as well as the number of values entered. After the user enters the sentinel value (–1), compute the average of the values based on the running total and the number of values entered. Display all three values — the total of the values entered, the number of values entered, and the average of the values — in the Console window using a user-friendly message. For example, test scores of 100, 95, 80, and 90 should produce the results shown in Figure 3-19.

FIGURE 3-19

4 Using a Two-Dimensional Array to Find Wind Chill Factors

Design and develop a program that accepts user input of a temperature between –20° F and 15° F and a wind velocity between 5 mph and 30 mph, both in multiples of five. Based on the user input, the program should look up the wind chill factor in a two-dimensional array and display it in the Console window along with a user-friendly message. Use a function procedure to find the result and then return the result to the calling event procedure. Use the following table of wind chill factors to calculate the wind chill.

Table of Wind Chill Factors

Temperature in Fahrenheit	WIND VELOCITY IN MILES PER HOUR					
	5	10	15	20	25	30
–20	–26	–46	–58	–67	–74	–79
–15	–21	–40	–51	–60	–66	–71
–10	–15	–34	–45	–53	–59	–64
–5	–10	–27	–38	–46	–51	–56
0	–5	–22	–31	–39	–44	–49
5	0	–15	–25	–31	–36	–41
10	7	–9	–18	–24	–29	–33
15	12	–3	–11	–17	–22	–25

In your program, initialize a two-dimensional array with the values from the table. After the user enters temperature and wind velocity, display the resulting wind chill factor in the Console window. Use a loop and a decision making statement to validate that each of the values entered by the user are valid and in the table.

Use the following sample data to test the program:

Temperature (°F)	Wind Velocity (mph)
–20	10
0	30
15	5

The output for the test data should be –46, –49, and 12, as shown in Figure 3-20.

FIGURE 3-20

C H A P T E R **4**

Windows Applications and Function Procedures

Objectives

You will have mastered the material in this chapter when you can:

- Create a Windows application
- Resize a form
- Change the property values of a form
- Add controls to a form
- Move and resize controls on a form
- Use the Label, NumericUpDown, TextBox, and Button controls

- Change the property values of controls
- Write the code for a Click event procedure
- Write and use a function in code

Introduction

As discussed in Chapter 1, Visual Basic .NET allows you to select from a number of different project types and templates so you can develop many different types of applications. The Commission Calculator programs developed in previous chapters were Console applications. Visual Basic .NET also includes the ability to create professional-looking Windows applications that use the graphical user interface of Windows. Figure 4-1a on the next page shows a Windows application running in the Windows operating system. The application performs the same task as the Commission Calculator program developed in Chapter 2, but uses a form, controls, and code to create an interface for the user to interact with the program. A **form** is a container for different components of the interface. During run time, a form is displayed as a window on the Windows desktop. **Controls** are the graphical elements that make up the interface. The form shown in Figure 4-1a shows four types of controls — Label controls, NumericUpDown controls, a TextBox control, and a Button control. Visual Basic .NET includes over 40 different types of controls that you can use to build an interface. Each control has a set of **properties** that define characteristics of the control, such as its background color or the text that is displayed on the control. Properties either can be changed at design time or changed in code during run time.

In many Windows applications, code designed to perform a task does not execute until the user takes some action, called an **event**. When an event occurs, such as a user clicking a button, then the code in that Button control's event procedure executes. An **event procedure** is a group of code statements triggered by an event. For this reason, Visual Basic .NET is said to be **event driven**. Figure 4-1b on the next page shows the code for a Button control's event procedure in lines 9 through 11. When the user clicks the Calculate Commission button, the code in the event procedure executes.

When the event procedure executes, it calls a function procedure, which is shown in lines 13 through 28 of Figure 4-1b. A **function procedure** is a block of code that performs a task and then returns a value to the line of code that called it. Function procedures allow you to place code that performs a specific calculation or task in a separate procedure so that the functionality is isolated and can be reused by other procedures. The CalculateCommission( ) function shown starting on line 13 performs the calculation of the commission using the code developed in Chapter 2. Line 28 then sends the resulting commission value back to the Button control's event procedure (line 10), which displays the value in the TextBox control by altering the text property of the TextBox control in line 10.

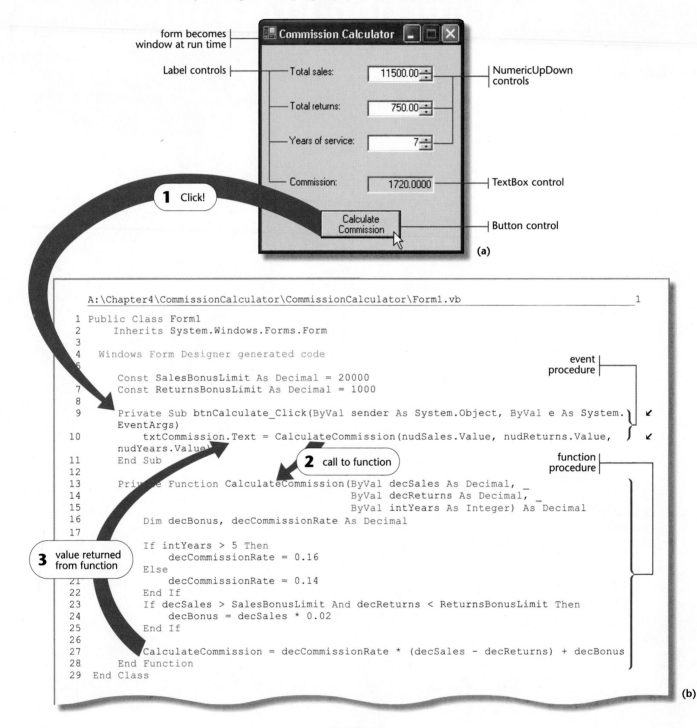

form becomes window at run time

Commission Calculator

Label controls

Total sales: 11500.00 — NumericUpDown controls

Total returns: 750.00

Years of service: 7

Commission: 1720.0000 — TextBox control

1 Click!

Calculate Commission — Button control

(a)

```
A:\Chapter4\CommissionCalculator\CommissionCalculator\Form1.vb                        1
1  Public Class Form1
2      Inherits System.Windows.Forms.Form
3
4   Windows Form Designer generated code
5
6      Const SalesBonusLimit As Decimal = 20000
7      Const ReturnsBonusLimit As Decimal = 1000
8
9      Private Sub btnCalculate_Click(ByVal sender As System.Object, ByVal e As System.
       EventArgs)
10         txtCommission.Text = CalculateCommission(nudSales.Value, nudReturns.Value,
       nudYears.Value)
11     End Sub
12
13     Private Function CalculateCommission(ByVal decSales As Decimal, _
14                                          ByVal decReturns As Decimal, _
15                                          ByVal intYears As Integer) As Decimal
16         Dim decBonus, decCommissionRate As Decimal
17
           If intYears > 5 Then
               decCommissionRate = 0.16
           Else
21             decCommissionRate = 0.14
22         End If
23         If decSales > SalesBonusLimit And decReturns < ReturnsBonusLimit Then
24             decBonus = decSales * 0.02
25         End If
26
27         CalculateCommission = decCommissionRate * (decSales - decReturns) + decBonus
28     End Function
29  End Class
```

event procedure

2 call to function

function procedure

3 value returned from function

(b)

FIGURE 4-1

After completing this chapter, you should be able to start a new Windows application project in Visual Basic .NET. You should be able to set properties for a form and add controls to a form. You also should be able to change control properties so that controls appear and behave in the manner you desire. You should be able to add event procedures to a control. Finally, you should be able to add a function procedure and call a function procedure within code.

Starting a New Windows Application

Starting a new Windows application uses steps similar to starting a new Console application, which you learned in Chapters 1 through 3. Instead of selecting the Console Application type, however, you select the Windows Application project type in the Templates list in the New Project dialog box. Figure 4-2 shows the New Project dialog box after entering the project name and selecting the Windows Application template.

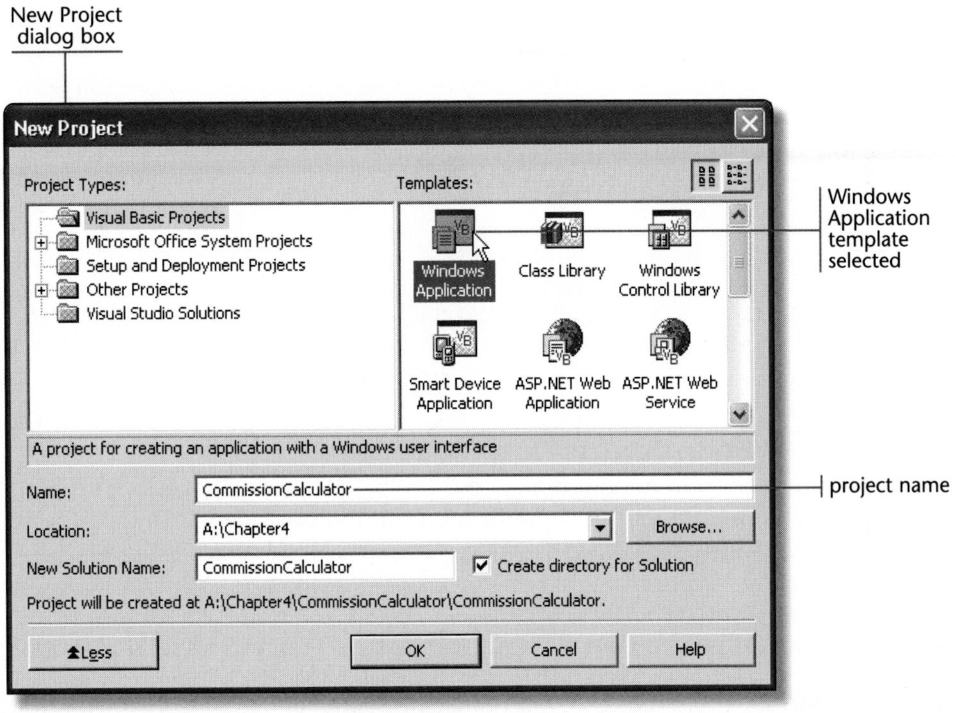

FIGURE 4-2

After the OK button is clicked in the New Project dialog box, Visual Basic .NET creates the new Windows Application project, named CommissionCalculator. Visual Basic automatically adds a new form to the project as shown in Figure 4-3 on the next page. At run time, the new form appears as the window in which the application runs. The form is contained in the Form1.vb file, as shown in the Solution Explorer window. A grid on the form allows you to align and size controls that are added to the form. **Sizing handles** that appear in white, such as those on the right and bottom sides of the form, allow you to change the size of the form. The sizing handles on the top and left side of the form, which appear in a light gray color, are nonfunctional.

The left side of the screen in Figure 4-3 shows the Toolbox window, or **Toolbox,** that contains all of the controls that you can add to the form. By default, the Toolbox window does not appear in the IDE. To display the Toolbox, click the Toolbox tab at the lower-left side of the IDE. When working on form design, however, you should keep the Toolbox docked at the left side of the IDE to make it easily accessible. To do so, click the Auto Hide button on the Toolbox title bar. You later can hide the Toolbox by clicking the Auto Hide button again.

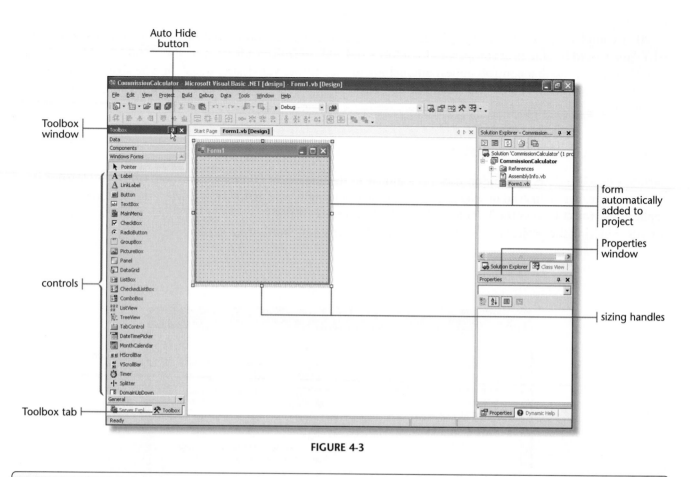

FIGURE 4-3

> **Best Practices**
>
> When working on form design, display the Toolbox. When you need more room in the IDE for such tasks as coding, use the Auto Hide button on the Toolbox title bar to hide the Toolbox.

Working with Form Properties for a Windows Application

Forms and controls include properties that you can change either at design time or run time. Properties are much like variables in that they have a name and a value. Changing the value of a property alters the appearance and behavior of the form or control in some way. This section discusses the most common properties of forms that you can change, in order to make a form appear and behave in a specific manner.

Form Properties

A number of form properties can be changed to define the appearance and behavior of a form. For example, the **Text property** of a form designates the text that appears on the form's title bar. In Figure 4-3, the Text property of the Form1 form is Form1, which is what currently is displayed on the form's title bar. Table 4-1 lists some of the most commonly used properties of a form, a description of each property, and the possible values for each property. The property value in bold is the default value for the property. The next section will discuss how to change the property values for a form.

Table 4-1 Form Properties

PROPERTY	DESCRIPTION	PROPERTY VALUES
BackColor	Sets the background color of application window	Any color selected from dialog box
ControlBox	Determines if a Windows control menu box (where icon is displayed) should appear on the form	**True** False
ForeColor	Sets the default color for text of controls that are added to the form	Any color selected from dialog box
FormBorderStyle	Dictates appearance of form border, whether the form is sizable, and how the Minimize and Maximize buttons, control menu box, and Help button behave	None FixedSingle Fixed3D FixedDialog **Sizable** FixedToolWindow SizableToolWindow
Icon	Defines the icon that is displayed in the control menu icon in the left corner of the window title bar and on the taskbar at run time	Any icon selected from a file dialog box
MaximizeBox	Determines if a Maximize button is displayed on the form's title bar	**True** False
MinimizeBox	Determines if a Minimize button is displayed on the form's title bar	**True** False
Size	Sets the width and height of the form in pixels	Two positive whole numbers, separated by a comma
StartPosition	Specifies the initial position of the form at the start of run time	CenterParent CenterScreen Manual WindowsDefaultBounds **WindowsDefaultLocation**
Text	Sets title to display on the title bar of application window	Any value
WindowState	Dictates how a window should be displayed initially during run time	**Normal** Minimized Maximized

Setting Form Properties for the Commission Calculator Program

During design time, form or control properties are set using the **Properties window**, which is displayed in the lower-right corner of the IDE as shown in Figure 4-3. Property names are listed in the left column of the Properties window (Figure 4-4 on the next page). The current property values are listed in the right column. The name of the selected control appears in the Object box at the top of the Properties window. To change a property value, you first select the property value that you want to change by clicking it and then change the property value. The way that you change the property value varies: some properties require you to select a value from a list, some allow you to type a new value, and others include an ellipse button that you click to display a dialog box from which you select a property value.

Figure 4-4 shows the form properties listed in alphabetical order. Clicking the Alphabetized button causes the properties to be listed in alphabetical order. By default, properties are sorted by category in Categorized view. Using the Categorized view displays the properties grouped into categories, such as Layout, Behavior, and Appearance. Clicking the Categorized button switches the sorting order to categorized.

Table 4-2 shows the property values that must be changed for the form in the Commission Calculator program.

If you are creating the Commission Calculator program, use the Properties window to change the property values listed in Table 4-2. As needed, use the scroll bar on the right side of the Properties window to find each property in the list. The StartPosition and FormBorderStyle properties utilize drop-down lists from which you can select the new value. When the FormBorderStyle property is changed, the form border is modified to reflect the change.

To change the values for the Size:Width and Size:Height properties, first use the lower-right sizing handle on the form to attempt to size the form properly. Then, check the property values in the Properties window to verify the sizes. An expand button (Figure 4-4) displayed next to the Size property name indicates that the property has subproperties that you can modify. In the case of the Size property, these subproperties are the Width and Height properties. To change these property values, you either can type 248,272 as the property value in the Size property to set the Width and Height property values to 248 and 272 respectively, or you can click the expand button next to the Size property and then type the individual values in the Width and Height properties.

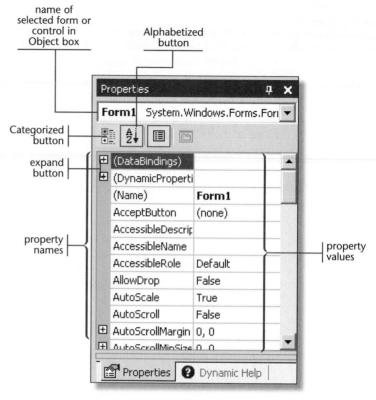

FIGURE 4-4

Table 4-2 Form Property Values for the Commission Calculator Program

PROPERTY	PROPERTY VALUE	EFFECT
FormBorderStyle	FixedDialog	Disallows resizing of the window at run time
Size:Width	248	Sets the width of the form in pixels
Size:Height	272	Sets the height of the form in pixels
StartPosition	CenterScreen	Causes the form to display in the center of the user's screen at the start of run time
Text	Commission Calculator	Sets the value to appear on the window's title bar

Working with Controls

When building a Windows application in Visual Basic .NET, you should use the following three-step method:

1. Create the interface
2. Set properties of the form and other controls
3. Write code

> **Best Practices**
>
> When building a user interface in Visual Basic .NET, you should use the following three-step method: 1) create the interface, 2) set properties of controls, and 3) write code.

In the first step, you should assemble components of the graphical user interface that will be used for obtaining input from the user and displaying output on one or more forms. Table 4-3 lists controls commonly used in Windows applications. The controls are listed in the order in which they appear in the Toolbox.

Table 4-3 Controls Commonly Used in Windows Applications

CONTROL NAME	DEFINITION
Label	Displays text that you do not want the user to be able to change during run time.
Button	Allows the user to initiate some event within the application during run time.
TextBox	Allows keyboard input during run time or displays text that the user can change during run time.
MainMenu	Provides a menu at the top of the form that can be customized during design time.
CheckBox	Creates a control that the user can check or uncheck by clicking it to indicate if something is true or false or to accept or reject some option presented.
RadioButton	Creates a radio button (also called an option button), several of which are grouped together to display a set of choices from which a single selection must be made.
GroupBox	Creates control used to contain, or group, other controls — typically RadioButtons.
PictureBox	Displays graphic images.
Panel	Creates a control used to contain, or group, other controls — typically used in dialog boxes.
ListBox	Displays a list of items from which the user can select one or more items. If the list is longer than the size of the list box, a scroll bar is added automatically.
ComboBox	Creates a combination list box and text box. The user can select either an item from the list or enter a value in the text box from the keyboard.
DateTimePicker	Displays a date and/or time that the user can modify by clicking a drop-down box arrow or up or down button.
MonthCalendar	Displays a highly customizable calendar that can allow the user to select a date, two or more dates, or date range.
HScrollBar	Displays a scroll bar that allows a user to scroll quickly left or right through a list of items. It can indicate the current position on a scale or it can be used as an input device.
VScrollBar	Performs the same functions as a horizontal scroll bar, but its orientation on the form is different, moving toward the top or bottom of the window.
Timer	Initiates an event at set intervals of time.
NumericUpDown	Allows input of numeric value and limits the range of values that the user can enter. The user can type a value or use up or down buttons to change the value in the control.
OpenFileDialog and other dialog controls	Creates the typical Open File dialog box used in Windows applications. This and other types of common dialog boxes can be customized and added to a form.

Adding Controls to a Form

Visual Basic .NET provides many methods for adding controls to a form. The following four methods are the most common methods of adding controls to a form.

1. Drag the control from the Toolbox to the form
2. Double-click the control in the Toolbox
3. Select the control in the Toolbox and then draw the control on the form
4. Select an existing control on a form, press CTRL+C to copy the control, and then press CTRL+V to paste a copy of the control on the form

The Commission Calculator program requires four types of controls: four Label controls, three NumericUpDown controls, one TextBox control, and one Button control (Figure 4-1a on page 80). The Label controls will identify the input and output controls to the user. For example, the first Label control will include the text, Total sales:, to indicate that the control to the right of the Label control is where the user inputs the total sales for a salesperson.

NumericUpDown controls will allow the user to input the three required numeric inputs values to the program — total sales, total returns, and years of service. A read-only TextBox control will display the output to the user. A Button control allows the user to initiate the commission calculation by clicking the button.

Figure 4-5 shows the Form1 form after adding the necessary controls. If you are creating the Commission Calculator program, add the nine controls using any of the four methods described above and position the controls in their approximate location, as shown in Figure 4-5. To find the NumericUpDown control in the Toolbox, use the scroll button in the lower-right corner of the Toolbox to scroll to the control. After adding the control, use the scroll button in the upper-right corner to scroll back to the top of the Toolbox.

As shown in Figure 4-5, the face of the Label, TextBox, and Button controls include text that represents the name of the control. Every control added to a form has a unique control name, which is a property of the control. The control name can be changed when the properties of the controls are set or left as the default.

When adding controls to a form, you should try to position them in their approximate final location. Later, when you change the properties of the controls, the size and position will be finalized so that the controls are aligned to create a professional-looking interface.

You also can resize a control on a form, move a control on a form, and delete a control from a form. To resize a control, select the control on the form

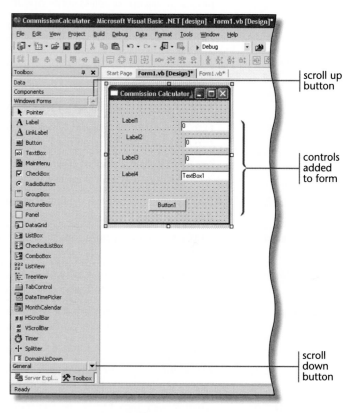

FIGURE 4-5

and then use the sizing handles on the border of the control. To move a control, drag the control from the current location to the new location on the form. When working with forms, you may find it is faster to add all of the required controls to the form and then position them correctly on the form. If you position individual controls before adding all the controls, you may have to reposition those controls to accommodate any additional controls.

> **Best Practices**
>
> When working with forms, you may find it is faster to add all of the required controls to the form and then position them correctly on the form.

To delete a control on a form, click the control to select it and then press the DELETE key. You also can select the control and click Delete on the Edit menu or right-click the control and then click Delete on the shortcut menu.

Controls and Control Properties

TextBox, Label, NumericUpDown, and Button controls often are used in a Windows application. These four controls can provide most of the input and output areas needed for an application's user interface. The property values for each control must be changed to position and size the controls correctly on the form and to define how users interact with the controls during run time. These controls will be discussed in detail in the following sections.

Common Properties of Controls

Many of the controls used in developing a Windows application share common properties. For example, the Form, TextBox, and Label controls, for example, all have Text, Size, and Location properties. Table 4-4 lists some of the more common properties of controls. The property value in bold is the default value for the property.

Table 4-4 Common Properties of Controls

PROPERTY	DESCRIPTION	PROPERTY VALUES
BackColor	Sets the background color of the control	Any color selected from dialog box
Enabled	If True, control is usable at run time; if False, a user cannot change control value and control may appear grayed out	**True** False
Font	Defines the text font to use if text is displayed in the control	Any font style selected from a dialog box
ForeColor	Changes the foreground color, usually of the text that is displayed on the control	Any color selected from dialog box
Location	Indicates the distance from the left and top border of the form in pixels	Two positive whole numbers, separated by a comma
Name	Provides a descriptive, unique identifier for the control	Any text
Size	Indicates the width and height of the control in pixels	Two positive whole numbers, separated by a comma
TabIndex	Determines the order in which the TAB key navigates to the control on the form	Any whole number
TabStop	Determines whether the TAB key sets focus on the control during run time	True False (default value varies by control)
Visible	If True, control appears at run time; if False, control does not appear or is dimmed	**True** False

Each of these controls also has a unique set of properties. Some of the unique properties of the TextBox, Label, NumericUpDown, and Button controls will be discussed in subsequent sections.

Label Control Properties

As you have learned, a Label control, as shown in Figure 4-1 on page 80, is used to display text on a form. During run time, the person using the application cannot change the text in a label. The important properties for a Label control include the Location, Size, Font, and Text properties. Table 4-5 lists several of the properties associated with the Label control, along with a brief description and a list of available property values.

Table 4-5 Label Control Properties

PROPERTY	DESCRIPTION	PROPERTY VALUES
FlatStyle	Determines the appearance of the control	Flat Popup **Standard** System
Image	Sets an image to be displayed on the visible portion of the Label control, along with the text set in Text property	Any picture selected from the hard drive using a dialog box
ImageAlign	If the Image property is set, sets the position within the label where the image is displayed	One of nine locations selected from a graphical map; default value is **MiddleCenter**
Text	Defines the visible text that displays on the control	Any text with any character length

Best Practices

Use Label controls to display text on a form that will not be modified at run time.

NumericUpDown Control Properties

A NumericUpDown control, as shown in Figure 4-1, allows the user to change an input value by typing it into the control, using the UP ARROW or DOWN ARROW keys on the keyboard, or using the mouse to click the up and down arrows. Table 4-6 lists several of the properties associated with the NumericUpDown control, with a brief description and a list of available property values. As shown in Table 4-6, the Value property defines the current value displayed in the control. The up and down arrows increase or decrease the value displayed in the control by a specific increment, as defined by the Increment property value. The Minimum property and Maximum property determine the range of allowable values. If the user enters a number outside of the range set by the Minimum and Maximum property values, the control automatically changes the entered number to the closest allowable value. The property values for the Value, Minimum, and Maximum properties can be integer or decimal values, depending on the value of the DecimalPlaces property. The DecimalPlaces property defaults to 0, to indicate that only integer values are accepted as input.

Best Practices

Use NumericUpDown controls for numeric input where you want to limit the range of allowed input values to fall between a minimum and maximum value.

Table 4-6 NumericUpDown Control Properties

PROPERTY	DESCRIPTION	PROPERTY VALUES
BorderStyle	Determines how the border of the NumericUpDown control is displayed	None FixedSingle **Fixed3D**
DecimalPlaces	Defines number of decimal places that are displayed in the value in the control	Any whole number from 0 to 99; default value is **0**
Increment	Defines amount to add or subtract from the displayed value each time user clicks the up or down arrow on control	Any positive number; default value is **1**
Maximum	Determines the highest allowable value in the control; if user enters a higher value, the value is set automatically to the Maximum value	Any number; default value is **100**
Minimum	Determines the lowest allowable value in the control; if user enters a lower value, the value is set automatically to the Minimum value	Any number; default value is **0**
TextAlign	Determines if text in the control is displayed left-aligned, right-aligned, or centered horizontally	**Left** Right Center
ThousandsSeparator	Determines if a Thousands separator character is used in the value, when appropriate; if True, the value is displayed with a thousands separator character that has been set on the user's system; if False, no thousands separator character is displayed	True **False**
UpDownAlign	Determines if the up and down arrows on the control are displayed on the left or right side of the control	Left **Right**
Value	Sets the value that is displayed in the control	Any value within the range set by the Minimum and Maximum property values

TextBox Control Properties

A TextBox control is used to allow a user to enter text during run time or displays text that the user can change during run time. A TextBox control has many properties used to define how the control is displayed on the form and how the user interacts with the control during run time. Table 4-7 on the next page lists several of the properties associated with the TextBox control, with a brief description and a list of available property values. The Height property, Width property, and Location property define the size and position of the TextBox control in the application window. The ReadOnly property determines whether or not the user can input data in the TextBox control at run time. The ReadOnly property value can be either True or False. The default value is False, meaning that users can input data in the TextBox control. When the ReadOnly property is set to True, the TextBox is grayed out, and the user is prevented from modifying the value of the control at run time.

Best Practices

Use TextBox controls for input and output values on a form that may change during run time.

Table 4-7 TextBox Control Properties

PROPERTY	DESCRIPTION	PROPERTY VALUES
AutoSize	Indicates whether the height of the control automatically changes when the font size of the text in the control is changed	**True** False
BorderStyle	Determines how the border of the TextBox control is displayed	None FixedSingle **Fixed3D**
MaxLength	Sets the maximum number of characters a user can input in the control	Any whole number from 0 through **32767**
Multiline	Determines if the text in the controls is displayed on more than one line	True **False**
ReadOnly	If True, a user cannot type or edit text in the control during run time; if False, a user can type and edit text in the control	True **False**
Text	Sets the text that is displayed inside the control	Any text with a character length up to the value specified in the MaxLength property
TextAlign	Determines if text in the control is displayed left-aligned, right-aligned, or centered horizontally	**Left** Right Center
WordWrap	If Multiline is True, text in control wraps to the next line when the text is longer than the width of the control	**True** False

Button Control Properties

Adding one or more Button controls to a user interface allows a user to indicate that the application should initiate an action, such as calculating a value based on inputs provided, resetting a value, or closing a window. Clicking the button causes the Click event procedure associated with the button to be executed. In the case of the Commission Calculator program, a Button control allows a user to tell the application to perform the calculation. Table 4-8 lists several of the properties associated with the Button control, with a brief description and a list of available property values.

Table 4-8 Button Control Properties

PROPERTY	DESCRIPTION	PROPERTY VALUES
FlatStyle	Determines the appearance of the control	Flat Popup **Standard** System
Image	Sets an image to be displayed on the visible portion of the Button control, along with the Text	Any picture selected from the hard drive using a dialog box
ImageAlign	If the Image property is set, determines where the image is displayed	One of nine locations selected from a graphical map; default is **MiddleCenter**
Text	Defines the visible text that is displayed on the control	Any text with any character length
TextAlign	Determines where text of the Text property value should be displayed on the button	One of nine locations selected from a graphical map; default is **MiddleCenter**

Setting Properties of Controls

To change a property value, you first select the property value that you want to change by clicking it and then changing the property value in the Properties window. When you click a control, the control name appears in the Object box at the top of the Properties window, and the list of properties is updated in the Properties list.

In creating the interface for the Commission Calculator program, property values for each of the nine controls added to the form must be changed, so that the controls appear and behave correctly at run time. For example, the text that is displayed on the face of the Label controls must be updated. The property values for the three NumericUpDown controls must be set to limit the user input to values in a specific range. The requirements are that the total sales be in a range from 0 to $50,000, the total returns in a range from 0 to $10,000, and the years of service in a range from 0 to 20 years.

Further, the Name property value of each control should be modified to give each control a meaningful name. While Visual Basic .NET gives each control a default name, it is preferable that more meaningful names be given to controls, especially those that are used for input and output. Just as with variables, it is beneficial to follow a standard naming convention for control names, based on the type of control. In this book, a three-character identifier will be used to prefix the control name. The following three-character prefixes can be used for TextBox, Label, NumericUpDown, and Button controls:

txt – TextBox controls
lbl – Label controls
nud – NumericUpDown controls
btn – Button controls

> **Best Practices**
>
> Use a standard naming convention when naming controls. For example, use three-character prefixes for control names, such as txt for TextBox controls, lbl for Label controls, nud for NumericUpDown controls, and btn for Button controls.

In addition to using a prefix, a control should be given a descriptive name so that programmers know the type of control that is being referenced in code. For example, if a NumericUpDown control will contain the years of service value, then the control can be named nudYears. Typically, because Label controls are not used for input and output, they are left with their default names.

Table 4-9 lists the control property values that must be changed in the Commission Calculator program.

Table 4-9 Control Property Values for the Commission Calculator Program

CONTROL	PROPERTY	VALUE	EFFECT
Label1	Location	32, 19	Indicates the distance from the left and top borders of the form in pixels
	Size	72, 24	Sets the width and height of the control in pixels
	Text	Total sales:	Sets Total sales: to be displayed as the initial value in the control at run time
Label2	Location	32, 59	Indicates the distance from the left and top borders of the form in pixels
	Size	72, 24	Sets the width and height of the control in pixels
	Text	Total returns:	Sets Total returns: to be displayed as the initial value in the control at run time

continued on the next page

Table 4-9 Control Property Values for the Commission Calculator Program (continued)

CONTROL	PROPERTY	VALUE	EFFECT
Label3	Location	32, 99	Indicates the distance from the left and top borders of the form in pixels
	Size	88, 24	Sets the width and height of the control in pixels
	Text	Years of service:	Sets Years of service: to be displayed as the initial value in the control at run time
Label4	Location	32, 147	Indicates the distance from the left and top borders of the form in pixels
	Size	72, 23	Sets the width and height of the control in pixels
	Text	Commission:	Sets Commission: to be displayed as the initial value in the control at run time
NumericUpDown1	DecimalPlaces	2	Sets the number of decimal places of the value to be displayed in the control
	Increment	1000	Causes the value in the control to increment or decrement by 1000 when the up or down arrows are clicked
	Location	128, 19	Indicates the distance from the left and top borders of the form in pixels
	Maximum	50000	Defines the highest value allowed in the control
	Name	nudSales	Changes the control's name to a descriptive name
	Size	80, 20	Sets the width and height of the control in pixels
	TextAlign	Right	Sets text to be displayed right-aligned in the control
NumericUpDown2	DecimalPlaces	2	Sets the number of decimal places of the value to be displayed in the control
	Increment	100	Causes the value in the control to increment or decrement by 100 when the up or down arrows are clicked
	Location	128, 59	Indicates the distance from the left and top borders of the form in pixels
	Maximum	10000	Defines the highest value allowed in the control
	Name	nudReturns	Changes the control's name to a descriptive name
	Size	80, 20	Sets the width and height of the control in pixels
	TextAlign	Right	Sets text to be displayed right-aligned in the control
NumericUpDown3	Location	128, 99	Indicates the distance from the left and top borders of the form in pixels
	Maximum	20	Defines the highest value allowed in the control
	Name	nudYears	Changes the control's name to a descriptive name
	Size	80, 20	Sets the width and height of the control in pixels
	TextAlign	Right	Sets text to be displayed right-aligned in the control
TextBox1	Location	128, 148	Indicates the distance from the left and top borders of the form in pixels
	Name	txtCommission	Changes the control's name to a descriptive name

Table 4-9 Control Property Values for the Commission Calculator Program (continued)

CONTROL	PROPERTY	VALUE	EFFECT
	ReadOnly	True	Prevents the user from entering a value in the control at run time; code can change text property at run time
	Size	80, 20	Sets the width and height of the control in pixels
	Text	<blank>	Sets the initial value in the control at run time to an empty string
	TextAlign	Right	Sets text to be displayed right-aligned in the control
Button1	Location	72, 188	Indicates the distance from the left and top borders of the form in pixels
	Name	btnCalculate	Changes the control's name to a descriptive name
	Size	96, 32	Sets the width and height of the control in pixels
	Text	Calculate Commission	Sets the text that is displayed on the button face to Calculate Commission

Figure 4-6 shows the Form1 form after the controls have been updated with the property values specified in Table 4-9 on pages 91 through 93. If you are creating the Commission Calculator program as shown in this chapter, select each control on the form and use the Properties window to set the control property values to those listed in Table 4-9.

Setting Additional Form and Control Properties

At run time, if a user wants to change a value in a specific input area, the user typically clicks the control used for that input area to select it. When a user selects a control, the control is said to have **focus**, and Visual Basic .NET places the insertion point in the control

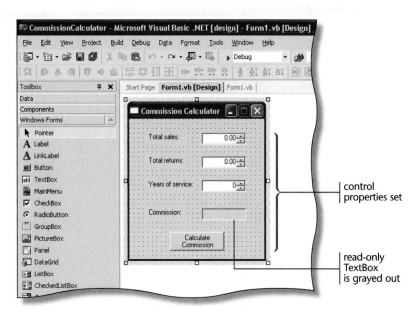

FIGURE 4-6

or displays a dotted rectangle around the control on the form. A user also can use the TAB key on the keyboard to select, or set, the focus on a specific control. Using the TAB key to set the focus on a control is called **tabbing**.

The TabIndex property determines the order in which Visual Basic .NET sets the focus on controls when a user presses the TAB key. When the application window first displays at run time, Visual Basic .NET will set the initial focus on the control with the lowest value for the TabIndex property, which is zero.

> **Best Practices**
>
> Take the time to fine-tune your user interface by setting such properties as the TabIndex and TabStop properties. Such detail is noticed by users and makes your program operate in a manner familiar to users of Windows applications.

In the Commission Calculator window, the NumericUpDown control used as the input area for total sales should have focus when the window first opens. Subsequent tabbing should set the focus on the total returns

NumericUpDown control, the years of service NumericUpDown control, and, finally, the Calculate Commission Button control. After the last control in the TabIndex sequence is reached, pressing the TAB key will restart the sequence and set the focus on the total sales NumericUpDown control. If you want Visual Basic .NET to skip a control during tabbing, you can change the value of its TabStop property from True to False.

While you can set the TabIndex and TabStop properties using the Properties window, Visual Basic .NET also provides graphical means to set these properties. When you click the Tab Order command on the View menu, Visual Basic .NET displays the TabIndex property value at the left corner of each control as shown in Figure 4-7a. You then click each property value in the order in which you want to set the tabbing order for the controls. That is, in the case of the CommissionCalculator form, first click the 4 in the top NumericUpDown control, then the 5, then the 6, and then the 8. Clicking the numbers in this order sets the tabbing order for the controls on the form as discussed above. Figure 4-7b shows the view of the form after setting the tabbing order. After setting the correct tabbing order for the CommissionCalculator form, click the Tab Order command on the View menu so that the numbers no longer appear and the tabbing order is set.

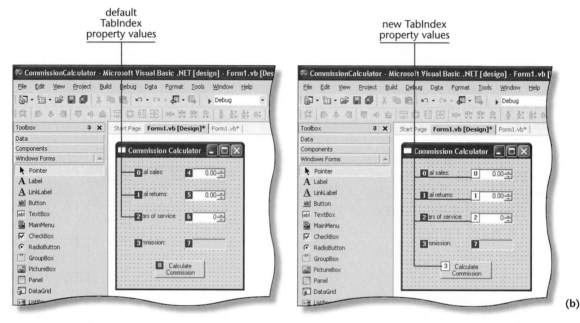

FIGURE 4-7

When a user enters values in a form using the keyboard, the user may find it inconvenient to move to the mouse in order to click a button to initiate an action. Typically, the user would like to press the ENTER key in order to initiate the action. You can set one button on a form to be the default accept button, which tells the application that pressing the ENTER key while focus is on any control on a form is the same as using the mouse to click the default accept button on the form. For the Commission Calculator program, the btnCalculate control should be the default accept button for the form. To indicate that a button is the default accept button, the form should be selected and then the AcceptButton property value must be set to the appropriate Button control (in this case, the btnCalculate control). After setting the AcceptButton property, the button designated as the AcceptButton is displayed with a black border around the button as shown in Figure 4-8. This provides a visual indication to the user that this button is the default accept button for the form.

> **Best Practices**
>
> Use the AcceptButton form property to designate a default button on a form. Use the CancelButton form property to designate a cancel or reset button on the form.

If you are creating the Commission Calculator program as shown in this chapter, follow the procedure outlined above to set the TabIndex property value for each control on the form and then to set the btnCalculate control to be the default accept button for the form.

With the final properties set, the interface for the Commission Calculator program is complete. The next section discusses the code written for the Commission Calculator interface.

Coding Events, Functions, and Procedures

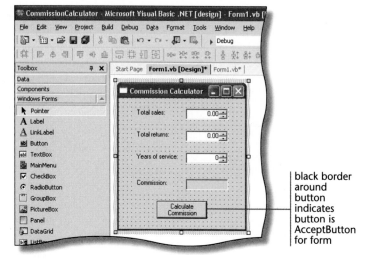

black border around button indicates button is AcceptButton for form

FIGURE 4-8

The third step in the Windows application development process is to write the code, or actions, that will occur in the application in response to specific events. As you have learned, events are messages sent to an object such as a control when the application runs. Events can be initiated when a user completes an action, such as clicking or dragging a control. Events also can be initiated by the application itself. As you have learned, events trigger event procedures, which are groups of code statements.

In Visual Basic .NET, certain controls are capable of recognizing events. For example, most types of Visual Basic .NET controls — including those that are displayed in the application window — recognize the Click event, which is an event initiated when the user clicks the left mouse button when the mouse pointer is over the control. Button controls are one type of control that can recognize the Click event. A control's name is used to associate an event with a specific control on a form, in order to tell Visual Basic .NET that an event initiated by that control should trigger the event procedure or code statements. For example, when the user clicks the left mouse button with the mouse pointer positioned on a specific Button control, such as btnCalculate, the code in the btnCalculate_Click event procedure executes.

A program that behaves as just described is called event driven. Code in event-driven programs executes only when a certain event, such as clicking a button, triggers the code to execute. Windows applications built using Visual Basic .NET are event driven.

Many times, the actions that you want to occur in the application in response to events can be expressed as changes in property values of controls on the form. The general form of a code statement used to change the value of a control property is:

controlname.propertyname = propertyvalue

where controlname is the name of the control, propertyname is the name of the property to change, and propertyvalue is the new value to which the property value should be changed.

Adding an Event Procedure for a Control

The Commission Calculator program requires you to add an event procedure for the Click event associated with the Calculate Commission button. To add an event procedure for the Button control, you double-click the control. Double-clicking a control opens the code window and automatically enters the first and last line of the event procedure. While a control may have many event procedures associated with it, only one event is the default event. For Button controls, the default event is the Click event. Double-clicking a Button control, therefore, creates a Click event procedure for the control.

Figure 4-9 on the next page shows the code window after double-clicking the Calculate Commission button on the form. Visual Basic .NET automatically created an event procedure (lines 164 through 166) to which you can

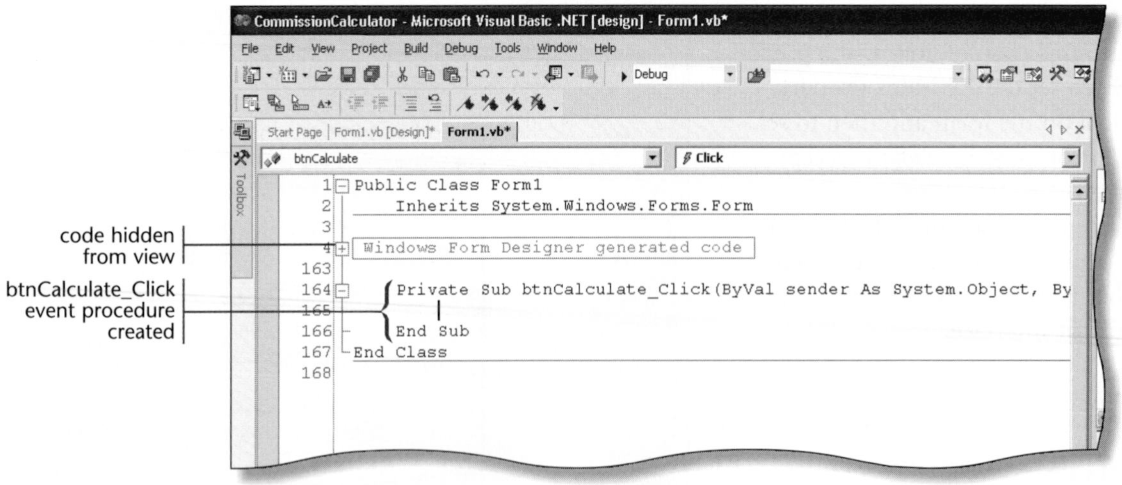

code hidden from view

btnCalculate_Click event procedure created

FIGURE 4-9

add code that executes when the user clicks the Calculate Commission button. Visual Basic .NET automatically created an event procedure (lines 164 through 169) that executes when the user clicks the Calculate Commission button during run time. As you created the interface for the program, Visual Basic .NET automatically inserted code in the code window. This code is hidden in line 4, and you never should modify or delete the hidden code. After the hidden code region, the line numbering continues at line 163. Clicking the plus sign exposes the hidden code region in the Code window. Hidden code regions are used to make coding easier by removing from view those sections of code with which you do not need to be concerned. The Toolbox has been hidden in Figure 4-9 by clicking the Auto Hide button on the Toolbox title bar so that more code can appear in the code window.

The calculation of the commission will be performed by a function procedure named CalculateCommission, which will be coded later in this chapter. The code for the btnCalculate_Click event procedure will call upon the CalculateCommission( ) function procedure, which will perform the calculation and then return the commission value to the event procedure. The event procedure then will place the commission value in the TextBox control named txtCommission. Figure 4-10 shows the code that must be added to the Commission Calculator program.

```
  3     ' Chapter 4:      Commission Calculator
  4     ' Programmer:     J. Quasney
  5     ' Date:           September 28, 2005
  6     ' Purpose:        This project calculates a salesperson's commissions
  7     '                 based on a commission percentage, total sales amount,
  8     '                 and total returns from customers. A bonus is calculated
  9     '                 based on years of service.
 10     '
 11     Windows Form Designer generated code
170
171     Const SalesBonusLimit As Decimal = 20000
172     Const ReturnsBonusLimit As Decimal = 1000
173
174     Private Sub btnCalculate_Click(ByVal sender As System.Object, ByVal e As System.   ↙
        EventArgs)
175         txtCommission.Text = CalculateCommission(nudSales.Value, nudReturns.Value,     ↙
        nudYears.Value)
176     End Sub
```

FIGURE 4-10

Figure 4-10 shows the comment block in lines 3 through 10. Lines 171 and 172 show the constant declarations to contain the values for the bonus limits. Line 175 shows the assignment statement that updates the Text property value of the TextBox control with the commission value calculated and returned by the CommissionCalculation() procedure. Updating the Text property value of the TextBox control causes the new value to appear to the user. The total sales, total returns, and years of service are parameters that are passed to the CommissionCalculation() procedure in the parentheses following the procedure name. The meanings of these parameters are discussed in the next section along with the coding of the CalculateCommission() procedure.

If you are coding the Commission Calculator program, a red or blue wavy line will appear below the CalculateCommission() procedure name because this procedure has not yet been coded. After coding the CalculateCommission() procedure, the wavy line will disappear.

If you are coding the CommissionCalculator program, enter lines 3 through 10 after line 2 in the code window. Then, enter lines 171 and 172 after line 170. Next, click the Form1.vb [Design] tab and double-click the Button control. After clicking the Button control, Visual Basic .NET automatically inserts the first and last line of the event procedure on lines 174 and 176. Finally, enter line 175 to complete the btnCalculate_Click event procedure.

Function Procedures

In Chapter 1 you learned about methods, such as the Console.Read() method, for performing specific tasks. You can code your own procedures to perform specific tasks and then call them in much the same way as you called the Console.Read() method. One type of procedure you can code is called a function procedure. As you have learned, a function procedure performs a task and then returns a value to the code that called it. Just as the Console.WriteLine() method accepted a parameter to tell the method what to write to the Console window, your function procedures also can accept parameters.

You should use function procedures in your code when your design calls for a specific calculation or operations that may be used several times in your code and whose end result is a single value, such as an Integer, Decimal, or Boolean result.

> **Best Practices**
> Use function procedures in your code when your design calls for a specific calculation or operations that may be used several times in your code and whose end result is a single value.

When adding a function procedure to your code, you first must declare the function and its data type, much as you declare an event procedure or variable. Table 4-10 shows the general form of a simple Function statement used to declare a function procedure and then write the code statements within the function procedure.

Table 4-10 Function Statement

General form:	1. Function name(argument 1, …, argument n) As datatype
	    statements
	End Function
	2. Private Function name(argument 1, …, argument n) As datatype
	    statements
	End Function
	where the Function name is a valid identifier that includes only letters, numbers, or the underscore character.

Purpose:	The Function statement declares a function procedure with arguments and a data type for the returned value.

continued on the next page

Table 4-10 Function Statement (continued)

Examples:	1. Function CalculateCommission() As Decimal

```
1. Function CalculateCommission() As Decimal
      .
      .
      .
         Return value
   End Function
2. Private Function CalculateCommission() As Decimal
      .
      .
      .
         CalculateCommission = value
   End Function
```

Notes: 1. The Private keyword used in Example 2 specifies that the function procedure is for use only by the code within the form. The Private keyword is optional, but it is good coding practice to specify it to make the code more understandable.

2. Arguments are optional. If used, arguments behave as local variables within the function procedure and are passed to the function procedure when it is called.

3. Arguments use the general form:
   Optional ByVal argumentname As datatype
   ByVal argumentname As datatype
   Optional ByRef argumentname As datatype
   ByRef argumentname As datatype
   The Optional keyword indicates that the arguments are not required when the procedure is called; they may be used when needed, or they may be omitted if not needed. The keywords, ByVal and ByRef, are beyond the scope of this book.

4. Assigning a value to the name of the function procedure as in Example 1 returns a value to the calling line of code when the function exits. Using the Return statement to return a value immediately causes the function to exit and return a value to the calling line of code.

You declare a function procedure as an array data type in much the same way that you declare variables arrays. For example, the function declaration

```
Private Function InventoryCounts() As Integer()
```

declares a function procedure that returns an array of integers.

Coding a Function Procedure

The Commission Calculator program uses a function procedure named CalculateCommission() to calculate a commission based on total sales, total returns, and years of service. Figure 4-11 shows the CalculateCommission() function procedure. The function declaration starts on line 178 and continues though line 180. The function is declared with the Decimal data type because the function returns a currency value. The three parameters represent the values that are passed to the function. Each parameter acts like a variable within the function, and each is declared with an appropriate data type. Because these parameters are declared in the function declaration, they do not need to be declared within the function itself.

The code on lines 181 through 194 is almost identical to the code used in Chapter 2. The main difference is that line 194 performs the calculation and then sets the result to the name of the function procedure — in this case, CalculateCommission(). When the function procedure ends execution, the function procedure returns whatever value was stored in the *CalculateCommission* variable within the function procedure. The function procedure, therefore, returns the commission value to the line of code that called the function.

```
178        Private Function CalculateCommission(ByVal decSales As Decimal, _
179                                    ByVal decReturns As Decimal, _
180                                    ByVal intYears As Integer) As Decimal
181            Dim decBonus, decCommissionRate As Decimal
182
183            ' Calculate the commission rate and bonus
184            If intYears > 5 Then
185                decCommissionRate = 0.16
186            Else
187                decCommissionRate = 0.14
188            End If
189            If decSales > SalesBonusLimit And decReturns < ReturnsBonusLimit Then
190                decBonus = decSales * 0.02
191            End If
192
193            ' Calculate the commission
194            CalculateCommission = decCommissionRate * (decSales - decReturns) + decBonus
195        End Function
```

FIGURE 4-11

If you are coding the Commission Calculator program, enter the code shown in Figure 4-11 after inserting a blank line after the End Sub statement in line 176. After the code in Figure 4-11 is added to the Commission Calculator program, the coding for the program is complete.

Saving, Testing, and Documenting the Commission Calculator Program

After the coding of the Commission Calculator Windows application is complete, the program should be saved and tested. The Save button on the Standard toolbar is used to save the program. This action saves both the form design and the code. To test the program, click the Start button on the Standard toolbar to execute the program. After entering test data and clicking the Calculate Commission button, the program displays the resulting commission, as shown in Figure 4-12. After testing the program, click the Close button on the window's title bar to halt execution of the program.

After saving and testing the code, the program should be documented by printing a hard copy of the program interface during run time and the program code.

To print a hard copy of the program code, follow the steps shown in Chapter 1 on page 20. Figure 4-13 on the next page shows the resulting printout of code.

As you learned in Chapter 1, Visual Basic .NET does not include functionality that allows you to print a program interface. Instead, you can follow the steps outlined in Chapter 1 on page 21 to press ALT+PRTSCR to take a picture of the screen display and then paste the image into Paint. Following those steps results in a printout that should show the Commission Calculator program as shown in Figure 4-12.

FIGURE 4-12

```
     A:\Chapter4\CommissionCalculator\CommissionCalculator\Form1.vb                    1

 1  Public Class Form1
 2      Inherits System.Windows.Forms.Form
 3      ' Chapter 4:      Commission Calculator
 4      ' Programmer:     J. Quasney
 5      ' Date:           September 28, 2005
 6      ' Purpose:        This project calculates a salesperson's commissions
 7      '                 based on a commission percentage, total sales amount,
 8      '                 and total returns from customers. A bonus is calculated
 9      '                 based on years of service.
10      '
11      Windows Form Designer generated code
12
13      Const SalesBonusLimit As Decimal = 20000
14      Const ReturnsBonusLimit As Decimal = 1000
15
16      Private Sub btnCalculate_Click(ByVal sender As System.Object, ByVal e As System.  ↙
        EventArgs)
17          txtCommission.Text = CalculateCommission(nudSales.Value, nudReturns.Value,    ↙
        nudYears.Value)
18      End Sub
19
20      Private Function CalculateCommission(ByVal decSales As Decimal, _
21                                  ByVal decReturns As Decimal, _
22                                  ByVal intYears As Integer) As Decimal
23          Dim decBonus, decCommissionRate As Decimal
24
25          ' Calculate the commission rate and bonus
26          If intYears > 5 Then
27              decCommissionRate = 0.16
28          Else
29              decCommissionRate = 0.14
30          End If
31          If decSales > SalesBonusLimit And decReturns < ReturnsBonusLimit Then
32              decBonus = decSales * 0.02
33          End If
34
35          ' Calculate the commission
36          CalculateCommission = decCommissionRate * (decSales - decReturns) + decBonus
37      End Function
38  End Class
39
```

FIGURE 4-13

Chapter Summary

In this chapter, you learned how to create a Windows application using Visual Basic .NET. You also learned how to add controls to a form and how to set properties of forms and controls. You learned about Label, TextBox, Button, and NumericUpDown controls. You also learned how to write code for event procedures. Finally, you learned how to create function procedures in code and call function procedures from other procedures.

Key Terms

Button (85)
CheckBox (85)
ComboBox (85)
controls (79)
DateTimePicker (85)

event (79)
event driven (79)
event procedure (79)
focus (93)
form (79)

function procedure (80)
GroupBox (85)
HScrollBar (85)
Label (85)
ListBox (85)

MainMenu (85)
MonthCalendar (85)
NumericUpDown (85)
OpenFileDialog (85)
Panel (85)
PictureBox (85)

Properties window (83)
property (79)
RadioButton (85)
sizing handles (81)
tabbing (93)
Text property (82)

TextBox (85)
Timer (85)
Toolbox (81)
VScrollBar (85)

Homework Assignments

Short Answer

1. Identify the elements shown in Figure 4-14.

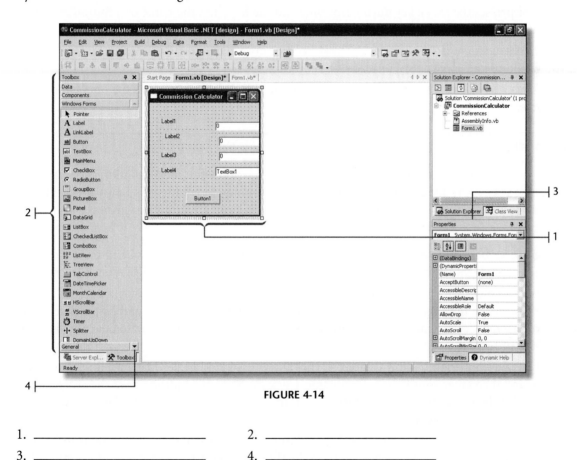

FIGURE 4-14

1. _____   2. _____
3. _____   4. _____

2. Describe the steps to delete a control from a form.
3. What does the following code display in the txtAverage1 and txtAverage2 TextBox controls.

```
dblAverage1 = (2.0 + 3.0 + 4.0 + 5.0) / 4.0
dblAverage2 = (12.0 + 24.0 + 36.0 + 48.0) / 4.0
txtAverage1.Text = dblAverage1
txtAverage2.Text = dblAverage2
```

4. The _____ property of a NumericUpDown control is displayed in the control. The _____ property of a form is displayed as the window title on the title bar at run time. The _____ property of a TextBox control is displayed in the control. The _____ property of a Label control is displayed in the control.

5. Write assignment code statements for the following:

    a. Assign the TextBox control named txtInventory the value 12

    b. Assign the NumericUpDown control nudAmount the value in the TextBox control txtAnswer1 plus 50

    c. Assign the TextBox control named txtResult the product of the values in the TextBox controls txtValue1 and txtValue2

    d. Triple the value in a TextBox control named txtAnswer3

    e. Assign the TextBox control named txtAnswer4 the quotient of the TextBox control named txtValue1 divided by the value in the NumericUpDown control named nudAnswer2

6. When the user presses the ENTER key during run time and the form has the name of a Button control assigned as the _____ property, the Click event procedure assigned to the button executes.

7. Describe when you would use a NumericUpDown control instead of a TextBox control for user input. Describe when you would use a Label control instead of a TextBox control.

8. Describe a situation where you may want a form to be resizable. What are some of the implications of making a form resizable?

Learn It Online

Instructions: To complete the Learn It Online exercises, start your browser, click the Address bar, and then enter the Web address scsite.com/progvb/learn. When the Programming Fundamentals Learn It Online page is displayed, follow the instructions in the exercises below. Each exercise has instructions for printing your results, either for your own records or for submission to your instructor.

1. **Chapter Reinforcement True/False, Multiple Choice, and Short Answer** Below Chapter 4, click the Chapter Reinforcement link. Print the quiz by clicking Print on the File menu for each page. Answer each question.

2. **Practice Test** Below Chapter 4, click the Practice Test link. Answer each question, enter your first and last name at the bottom of the page, and then click the Grade Test button. When the graded practice test is displayed on your screen, click Print on the File menu to print a hard copy. Continue to take practice tests until you score 80% or better.

3. **Crossword Puzzle Challenge** Below Chapter 4, click the Crossword Puzzle Challenge link. Read the instructions, and then enter your first and last name. Click the SUBMIT button. Work the crossword puzzle. When you are finished, click the Submit button. When the crossword puzzle is redisplayed, click the Print Puzzle button to print a hard copy.

4. **Tips and Tricks** Below Chapter 4, click the Tips and Tricks link. Click a topic that pertains to Chapter 4. Right-click the information and then click Print on the shortcut menu. Construct a brief example of what the information relates to in Visual Basic .NET to confirm you understand how to use the tip or trick.

5. **Newsgroups** Below Chapter 4, click the Newsgroups link. Click a topic that pertains to Chapter 4. Print three comments.

6. **Expanding Your Horizons** Below Chapter 4, click the Expanding Your Horizons link. Click a topic that pertains to Chapter 4. Print the information. Construct a brief example of what the information relates to in Visual Basic .NET to confirm you understand the contents of the article.

7. **Search Sleuth** Below Chapter 4, click the Search Sleuth link. To search for a term that pertains to this chapter, select a term below the Chapter 4 title and then use the Google search engine at google.com (or any major search engine) to display and print two Web pages that present information on the term.

Programming Assignments

1 Designing a Visual Basic .NET Application

At Barry's Electronics, salespersons receive a commission rate that ranges from 5% (.05) to 15% (.15) on home electronic sales in increments of .5% (.005), depending on the sale price. Design a Windows application that accepts the sale price and a commission rate as inputs. The application should calculate and display the resulting commission and allow the user to reset the input and output values. The formula for calculating the commission is:

Commission = SalesPrice × CommissionRate

Perform the following tasks to design a solution to the problem.

a. On paper, design a suitable user interface for the application. Be as specific as possible in naming controls and specifying their functions.

b. List all properties and property values for the form and any controls that the application requires. You need to list only those properties that must be changed from their default values.

c. On paper, write pseudocode for any events that need to be coded, based on your design in Step a above.

d. Desk-check your design by testing your application on paper. Draw a three-column table with the two input values in columns 1 and 2, and the output value in column 3. Create three rows that contain various input values for the item sale price and commission rate. Test your program design by substituting the values in columns 1 and 2 into your pseudocode. Write the results in column 3. Double-check the values against the formula in the instructions to make certain the pseudocode properly solves the problem.

e. Use Visual Basic .NET to implement the design in a new Windows application.

2 Money Changer

Design and develop a Windows application that will make change for a one-dollar bill on a sale of less than or equal to one dollar. The program should accept user input with a range from 1 cent to 100 cents, where the user can enter the amount of the sale. The program should determine the number of half dollars, quarters, dimes, nickels, and pennies to be returned to the customer. Develop the program logic to return as many half dollars as possible, then as many quarters as possible, and so on. For example, the output for a sale of $0.74 should be 0 Half Dollar, 0 Quarter, 2 Dime, 1 Nickels, and 1 Penny. After the change has been determined, the program should display the values to the user. The application should include one NumericUpDown control for user input and five read-only TextBox controls for the output values. Include one Button control that initiates the calculation. Place the logic for the calculation in the Button control's Click event procedure. Figure 4-15 shows the result of making change for a 6-cent purchase.

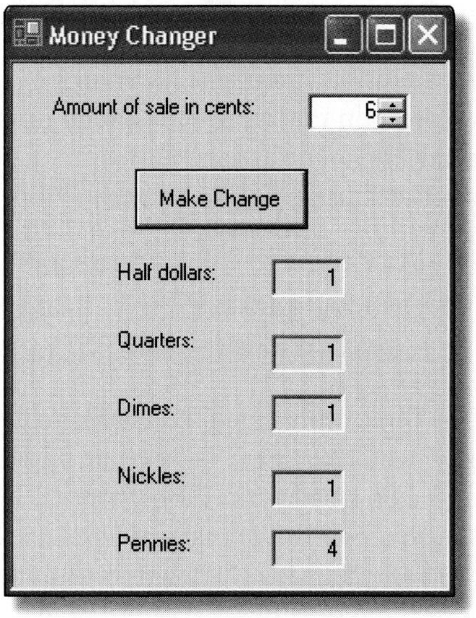

FIGURE 4-15

3 Future Value Calculation

Design and develop a Windows application that will perform the future value
calculation described in Programming Assignment 4 in Chapter 1 on page 28.
The application should include three NumericUpDown controls that accept the
input values. The allowed range for the investment should be a whole number
between 1 and 100,000. The allowed range for the interest rate should be a decimal value with two decimal places between 1.00 and 10.00. The allowed range for
the years should be a whole number between 2 and 10. Use a Button control to
initiate the calculation. Place the logic for the calculation in a function that
returns a decimal value and display the result in a read-only TextBox control.
Figure 4-16 shows the future value of a $100,000 investment at 5.5% after 5 years.

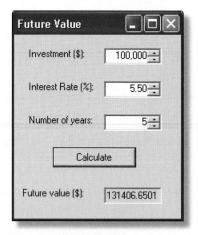

FIGURE 4-16

4 Rule of Thumb Calculation

Design and develop a Windows application that will perform
the tailor's rule of thumb calculations described in
Programming Assignment 2 in Chapter 1 on page 27. Place
each of the three calculations in separate functions. Use
appropriate controls to accept input and display results. Use a
Button control to allow the user to reset the values in the
input and output controls to their default values. Use proper
tabbing order, and set a Button control as the default button
for the form. Assign the Reset button to be the form's cancel
button. A weight of 120 pounds and a waistline of 30 inches
should result in a neck size of 4, a hat size of 6, and a shoe
size of 12, as shown in Figure 4-17.

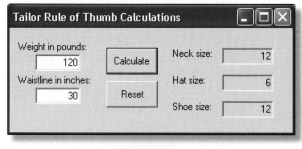

FIGURE 4-17

5 Computing Financial Ratios

As an intern at a financial services company, you have been asked to develop an
application that computes several fundamental financial ratios based on readily
available financial data. Ratios are the result of one financial value divided by
another financial value. The equations for the required ratios are:

- Price earnings ratio = Market price per share/Earnings per share
- Dividend payout ratio = Dividends per share/Earnings per share
- Dividend yield ratio = Dividends per share/Market price per share

The three inputs required are Market price per share, Earnings per share, and
Dividends per share. Develop an application that accepts the necessary inputs
and then displays the ratios. Include a Reset button to set the values back to 0 in
the window. Use at least one TextBox control, at least one Button control, and at
least one NumericUpDown control in the application. Use proper tabbing
order, and set a Button control as the default button for the form. Figure 4-18
shows the resulting financial ratios for a company with a stock price of $25.00,
earnings per share of $2.00, and a dividend of 50 cents.

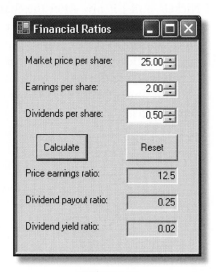

FIGURE 4-18

APPENDIX
A

Flowcharting and Pseudocode

Appendix A explains how to prepare, use, and read program flowcharts and pseudocode. Chapter 1 includes an introduction to flowcharting and flowchart symbols beginning on page 4. Pseudocode is introduced in Chapter 2 on page 31.

Guidelines for Preparation of Flowcharts

Before the flowchart can be drawn, a thorough analysis of the problem, the input data, and the desired output results must be performed. The program logic required to solve the problem also must be determined. On the basis of this analysis, a **general flowchart** illustrating the main path of the logic can be sketched. The general flowchart can be refined until the overall program logic is determined fully. This general flowchart is used to make one or more **detailed flowcharts** of the various branches of and detours from the main path of the program logic. After each detailed flowchart has been freed of logical errors and other undesirable features, such as unnecessary steps, the actual coding of the program in a computer language can be undertaken.

Straight-Line Flowcharts

Figure A-1 illustrates a general, **straight-line flowchart**. A straight-line flowchart is one in which the symbols are arranged sequentially, without any deviations or looping, until the terminal symbol that represents the end of the flowchart is reached. Once the operation indicated in any one symbol has been performed, that operation is never repeated.

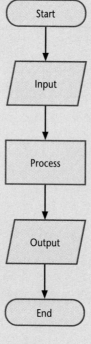

FIGURE A-1

Flowcharts with Looping

A general flowchart that illustrates an iterative, or repeating, process known as **looping** is shown in Figure A-2. The logic illustrated by this flowchart is in three major parts: initialization, process, and wrap-up. A flowline exits from the bottom symbol in Figure A-2 and enters above the diamond-shaped decision symbol that determines whether the loop is to be executed again. This flowline forms part of a loop in which the input, process, and output pattern is executed repeatedly until specified conditions are satisfied. The decision symbol shows where the decision is made to continue or stop the looping process and then perform the wrap-up operations.

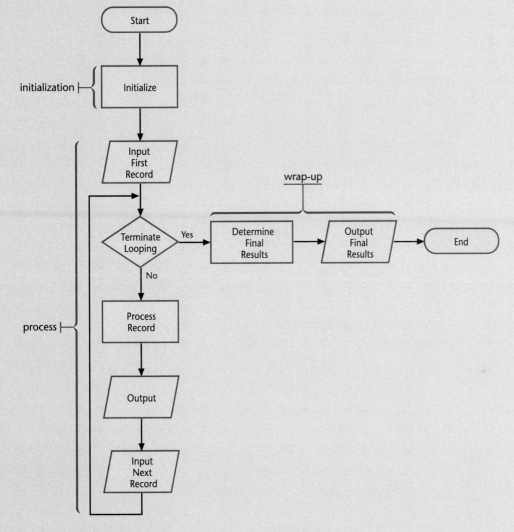

FIGURE A-2

Figure A-2 contains three braces that show how the flowchart represents the initialization, process, and wrap-up operations. For example, setting the program counters to 0 can represent an initialization operation and displaying the values of counters can represent a wrap-up operation.

Like the straight-line flowchart, a flowchart with looping need not have all the symbols shown in Figure A-2, or a flowchart can have many more symbols. For example, the process symbol within the loop in Figure A-2, when applied to a particular problem, can expand to include branching forward to bypass a process or backward to redo a process. It also is possible that through the use of decision symbols, the process symbol in Figure A-2 could be expanded to include several loops, some of which might be independent from each other and some of which might be within other loops.

A flowchart shows a process that is carried out. Flowcharts are flexible; they can show any logical process no matter how complex it may be, in whatever level of detail is needed. For example, the two flowcharts illustrated in Figure A-3 represent the same program that accepts and then displays a record. Then the program loops back to the accepting operation and repeats the sequence, accepting and displaying any number of records. In the flowchart on the right, a connector symbol, represented by a circle with a letter or number in it (in this case, A), indicates the continuation of the looping process.

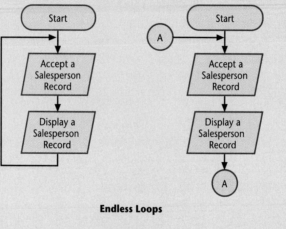

Endless Loops

FIGURE A-3

Although the flowcharts in Figure A-3 illustrate two ways a loop can be represented, the particular loop that is shown is an **endless loop**, also called an **infinite loop**. This type of loop should be avoided when constructing programs. In order to make a program finite, you must define it so it will terminate when specified conditions are satisfied.

Figure A-4 illustrates the use of a counter that terminates the looping process. Note that the counter first is set to 0 in the initialization step. After an account is read and a message is printed, the counter is incremented by 1 and tested to find whether it now is equal to 15. If the value of the counter is not 15, the looping process continues. If the value of the counter is 15, the looping process terminates.

For the flowchart used in Figure A-4, the exact number of accounts to be processed must be known beforehand. In practice, this always will not be the case, because the number of accounts may vary from one run to the next.

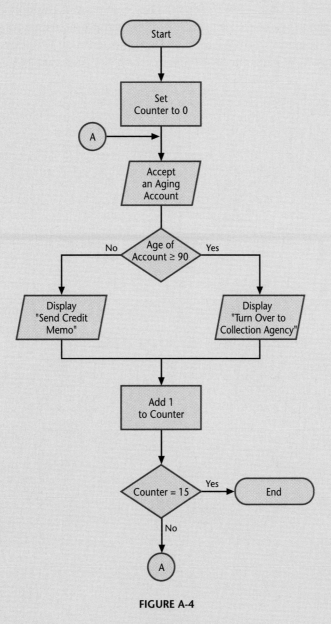

FIGURE A-4

A way to solve this type of problem is shown in Figure A-5, which illustrates the use of an end-of-file test to terminate the looping process. The value –999999 has been chosen to be the last account number. This kind of value sometimes is known as the **sentinel value** because it guards against continuing past the end-of-file. Also, the numeric item chosen for the last value cannot possibly be confused with a valid item because it is outside the range of the account numbers. Programs using an end-of-file test, such as the one shown in Figure A-5, are far more flexible and less limited than programs that do not, such as those illustrated in Figure A-3 on page 108 and Figure A-4 on the previous page.

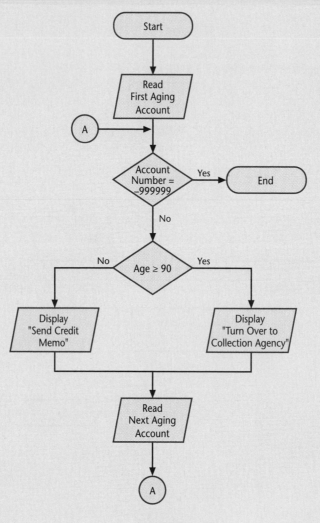

FIGURE A-5

Figure A-6 shows another flowchart with a loop. The loop represented by the flowchart illustrates the concept of counting and the use of the end-of-file test.

Simple computer programs do not require complex flowcharts and sometimes do not require flowcharts at all. As programs become more complex with many different paths of execution, however, a flowchart not only is useful, but usually is a prerequisite for successful analysis and coding. Indeed, developing the problem solution by arranging and rearranging the flowchart symbols can lead to a more efficient solution.

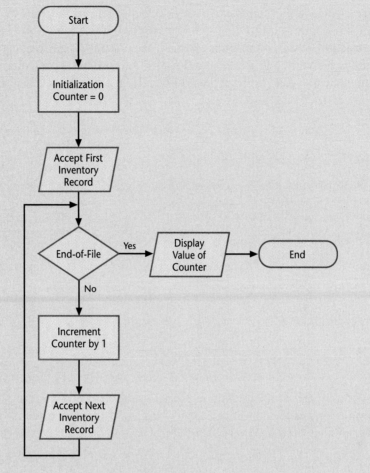

FIGURE A-6

Control Structures

The logic of almost any procedure or method can be constructed from the following three basic control structures:

1. Sequence
2. If...Then...Else or Selection
3. Do While or Repetition

The following are two common extensions to these control structures:

Do Until
Select Case (an extension of the If...Then...Else control structure)

The **Sequence structure** is used to show one action or one action followed by another, as illustrated in Figures A-7a and A-7b. Every flowchart in this book includes this control structure.

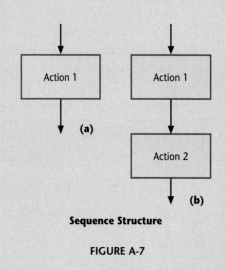

Sequence Structure

FIGURE A-7

The **If...Then...Else structure** represents a two-way decision made in the logic of the program. The decision is made on the basis of a condition that must be satisfied. If the condition is not satisfied, the program logic executes one action. If the condition is satisfied, the program logic executes a different action. This type of control structure is shown in Figures A-8a and A-8b. The flowcharts presented in Figures A-4 and A-5 on pages 109 and 110 include this control structure. The If...Then...Else structure also can result in a decision to take no action, as shown in Figure A-8b.

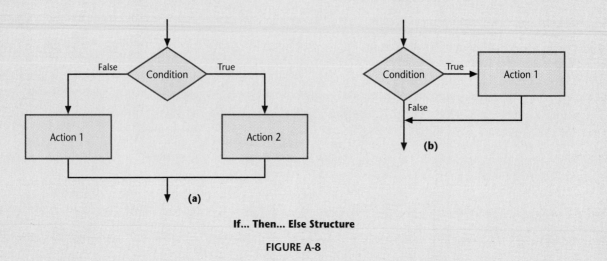

If... Then... Else Structure

FIGURE A-8

The **Do While structure** is the control structure most commonly used to create a process that will repeat as long as the condition is true. The Do While structure is illustrated in Figure A-9 and has been used earlier in Figures A-2 on page 107, A-5 on page 110, and A-6 on the previous page. In a Do While structure, the decision to perform the action within the structure is at the top of the loop; as a result, the action will not occur if the condition is never satisfied.

The **Do Until structure** also is used for creating a process that will be repeated. The major differences between the Do Until and the Do While structures are that (1) the action within the structure of a Do Until always will be executed at least once, (2) the decision to perform the action within the structure is at the bottom of the Do Until loop, and (3) the Do Until loop exits when the condition is true. The flowchart in Figure A-10 illustrates the Do Until structure; the flowchart presented in Figure A-4 also includes a Do Until structure.

The **Select Case structure** is similar to the If...Then...Else structure except that it provides more than two alternatives. Figure A-11 illustrates the Select Case structure.

A logical solution to a programming problem can be developed through the use of just these five control structures. The program will be easy to read, easy to modify, and reliable; most important of all, the program will do what it is intended to do.

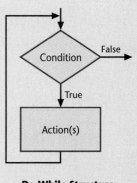

Do While Structure

FIGURE A-9

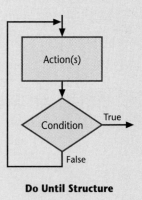

Do Until Structure

FIGURE A-10

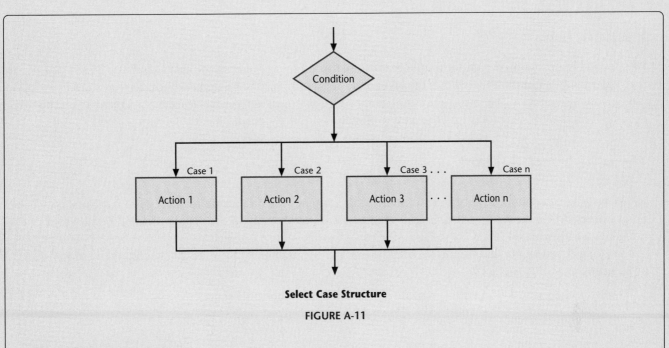

Select Case Structure

FIGURE A-11

Flowcharting Tips

The following recommendations can help make flowcharts more efficient and easier for others to understand. These suggestions assume that the input, processing, and output of the problem are defined properly in a requirements document.

1. Sketch a general flowchart and the necessary detail flowcharts before coding the problem. Repeat this step until you are satisfied with your flowcharts.
2. Use the control structures described on pages 111 and 112.
3. Put yourself in the position of the reader, keeping in mind that the purpose of the flowchart is to improve the reader's understanding of the solution to the problem.
4. Show the flow of processing from top to bottom and from left to right. When in doubt, use arrowheads as required to indicate the direction of flow.
5. Draw the flowchart so it is neat and clear. Use the connector symbols to avoid excessively long flowlines.
6. Choose labels for each symbol that explain the function of the symbols in a clear and precise manner.
7. Avoid endless loops; construct loops so they will be terminated when specific conditions are satisfied.

The reason that flowcharts are so important is simple: the difficulties in programming lie mostly in the realm of logic, not in the syntax and semantics of the computer language. In other words, most computer errors are mistakes in logic. A flowchart aids in detecting these types of mistakes.

Pseudocode

Pseudocode is a program design technique that uses natural English and resembles Visual Basic .NET code. It is an intermediate notation that allows the logic of a program to be formulated without diagrams or charts. Pseudocode resembles Visual Basic .NET in that specific operations can be expressed as commands that the program will execute. The following three examples illustrate pseudocode:

Accept Employee Record
MaleCounter = MaleCounter +1
Display Employee Record

What makes pseudocode appealing to many programmers is that it has no formal syntax, which allows programmers to concentrate on the design of the program rather than on the peculiarities of the programming language's syntax.

Although pseudocode has no formal rules, the following guidelines commonly are accepted by most programmers:

1. Begin the pseudocode with a program, procedure, or method title statement.

    Monthly Sales Analysis Report Procedure

2. End the pseudocode with a terminal program statement.

    End

3. Begin each statement on a new line. Use simple and short imperative sentences that contain a single transitive verb and a single object.

    Accept EmployeeNumber
    Subtract 10 From Quantity

4. Express assignments as a formula or as an English-like statement.

    WithholdingTax = 0. 20 $\times$ (GrossPay $-$ 38.46 $\times$ Dependents)

    or

    Compute WithholdingTax

5. To avoid errors in the design, avoid using logic structures not available in the programming language being used.

6. For the If…Then…Else structure, use the following conventions:

    a. Indent the true and false tasks.

    b. Use End If as the structure terminator.

    c. Vertically align the If, Else, and End If statements.

    These conventions for the If…Then…Else structure are illustrated in Figures A-12 and A-13.

```
If Balance < 500 Then
        Display Credit OK
Else
        Display Credit not OK
End If
```

FIGURE A-12

```
If GenderCode = male Then
        MaleCount = MaleCount + 1
        If Age > 21 Then
                MaleAdultCount = MaleAdultCount + 1
        Else
                MaleMinorCount = MaleMinorCount + 1
        End If
Else
        FemaleCount = FemaleCount + 1
        If Age > 21 Then
                FemaleAdultCount = FemaleAdultCount + 1
        Else
                FemaleMinorCount = FemaleMinorCount + 1
        End If
End If
```

FIGURE A-13

7. For the Do While structure, use the following conventions:

    a. If the structure represents a counter-controlled loop, begin the structure with Do.

    b. If the structure does not represent a counter-controlled loop, begin the structure with Do While.

    c. Specify the condition on the Do While or Do line.

    d. Use End Do as the last statement of the structure.

    e. Align the Do While or Do and the End Do vertically.

    f. Indent the statements within the loop.

    The conventions for the Do While structure are illustrated in Figures A-14 and A-15.

8. For the Do Until structure, use the following conventions:

    a. Begin the structure with Do Until.

    b. Specify the condition on the Do Until line.

    c. Use End Do as the last statement of the structure.

    d. Align the Do Until and the End Do vertically.

    e. Indent the statements within the loop.

    The conventions for the Do Until structure are illustrated in Figure A-16.

```
SumFirst100Integers Procedure
        Sum = 0
        Do Integer = 1 to 100
                Sum = Sum + Integer
        End Do
        Display sum
End
```

FIGURE A-14

```
EmployeeFileList Procedure
        Display report and column headings
        EmployeeCount = 0
        Accept first Employee record
        Do While Not End-of-File
                Add 1 to EmployeeCount
                Display Employee record
                Accept next Employee record
        End Do
        Display EmployeeCount
End
```

FIGURE A-15

```
SumFirst100Integers Procedure
        Sum = 0
        Integer = 1
        Do Until Integer >100
                Sum = Sum + Integer
                Integer = Integer + 1
        End Do
        Display Sum
End
```

FIGURE A-16

9. For the Select Case structure, use the following conventions:

   a. Begin the structure with Select Case, followed by the variable to be tested.

   b. Use End Case as the last statement of the structure.

   c. Align Select Case and End Case vertically.

   d. Indent each alternative.

   e. Begin each alternative with Case, followed by the value of the variable that equates to the alternative.

   f. Indent the action of each alternative.

These conventions are illustrated in Figure A-17.

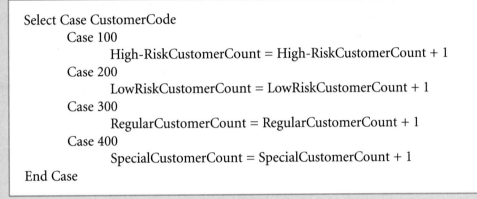

```
Select Case CustomerCode
        Case 100
                High-RiskCustomerCount = High-RiskCustomerCount + 1
        Case 200
                LowRiskCustomerCount = LowRiskCustomerCount + 1
        Case 300
                RegularCustomerCount = RegularCustomerCount + 1
        Case 400
                SpecialCustomerCount = SpecialCustomerCount + 1
End Case
```

FIGURE A-17

For an additional example of pseudocode, see Figure 2-5 in Chapter 2 on page 33.

Homework Assignments

1. In the flowchart in Figure A-18, what are the value of *I* and the value of *J* at the instant just after the statement *J* = *J* + 1 is executed for the fifth time? The value of *I* and *J* after the statement *I* = *I* + 2 is executed the tenth time? (A statement such as *J* = *J* + 1 is valid and is read as the new value of *J* equals the old value of *J* plus one or, equivalently, the value of *J* is to be replaced by the value of *J* plus one.)

2. Consider the section of a flowchart shown in Figure A-19. It assumes that an absent-minded person is going to work. This individual usually has the car keys but occasionally forgets them. Does the flowchart section in Figure A-19 incorporate the most efficient method of representing the actions to be taken? If not, redraw the flowchart portion given in Figure A-19.

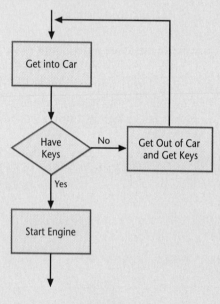

FIGURE A-19

3. In Figure A-20, the flowchart for a small program, what values of *I* and of *J* are printed when the output symbol is executed for the fiftieth time?

4. An opaque urn contains three diamonds, four rubies, and two pearls. Construct a flowchart that describes the following events: Take a gem from the urn. If it is a diamond, lay it aside. If it is not a diamond, return it to the urn. Continue in this fashion until all the diamonds have been removed. After all the diamonds have been removed, repeat the same procedure until all the rubies have been removed. After all the rubies have been removed, continue in the same fashion until all the pearls have been removed.

5. In the flowchart represented by Figure A-21, what is the value of *I* and the value of *J* at the instant the terminal symbol with the word, End, is reached?

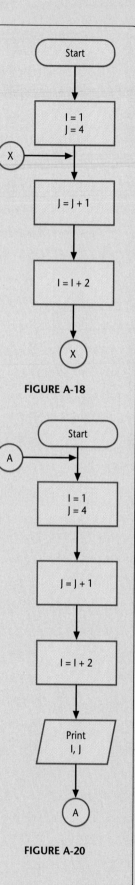

FIGURE A-18

FIGURE A-20

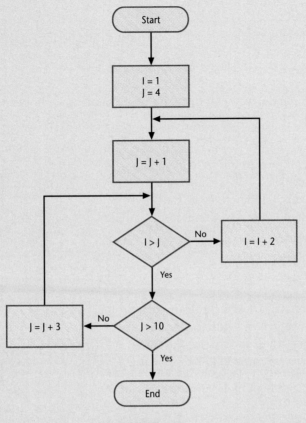

FIGURE A-21

6. Draw one flowchart, and only one, that will cause the mechanical mouse[1] to go through any of the four mazes shown in Figure A-22. At the beginning, a user will place the mouse on the Entry side of the maze, in front of the entry point, facing up toward the maze. The instruction *Move to next cell* will put the mouse inside the maze. Each maze has four cells. After that, the job is to move from cell to cell until the mouse emerges on the Exit side. If the mouse is instructed to Move to next cell when a wall is in front of it, it will hit the wall and fall apart. Obviously, the mouse must be instructed to test whether it is *Facing a wall* before any *Move*. The physical movements and logical tests the mechanical mouse can complete are listed on the next page.

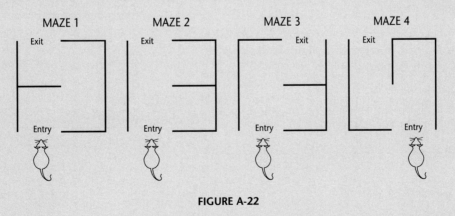

FIGURE A-22

[1] Special thanks to Dr. John Maniotes of Purdue University for his contribution to the mechanical mouse and mechanical man exercises.

a. Physical movement:

(1) Move to next cell. (The mouse will move in the direction it is facing.)

(2) Turn right.

(3) Turn left.

(4) Turn around 180 degrees. (All turns are made in place, without moving to another cell.)

(5) Halt.

b. Logic:

(1) Facing a wall? (Through this test, the mouse determines whether a wall is immediately in front of it, that is, on the border of the cell it is occupying and in the direction it is facing.)

(2) Outside the maze?

(3) On the Entry side?

(4) On the Exit side?

7. A flowchart representation of part of a cardiovascular disease risk assessment is shown in Figure A-23. The higher the point total, the greater the risk. In the spaces provided, write the point total for the following persons.

1. A 25-year old smoker with high blood pressure who eats a low fat diet.

_____

2. A 35-year old non-smoker with normal blood pressure who eats a low fat diet.

_____

3. A 20-year old non-smoker with high blood pressure who eats a high fat diet.

_____

4. A 45-year old smoker with high blood pressure who eats a high fat diet.

_____

5. A 61-year old non-smoker with high blood pressure who eats a high fat diet.

_____

6. A 16-year old non-smoker with normal blood pressure who eats a high fat diet.

_____

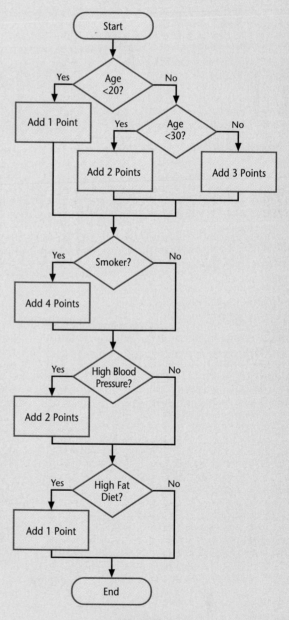

FIGURE A-23

8. Draw one flowchart that enables the mechanical man to accomplish the objectives efficiently in both Phase 1 and Phase 2, as illustrated in Figure A-24 (see note 1 on page 119).

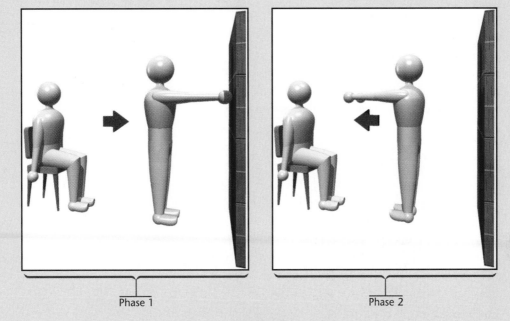

FIGURE A-24

The mechanical man possesses the following properties:

1. He is restricted to a limited set of operations.

2. He is event-driven (doing nothing unless given a specific instruction).

3. He must carry out instructions one at a time.

4. He understands the following instructions:

    a. Physical movement:

        (1) Stand

        (2) Sit

        (3) Take one step forward

        (4) Raise arms straight ahead

        (5) Lower arms to sides

        (6) Turn right (90 degrees without taking a step)

    b. Arithmetic:

        (1) Add one to a running total

        (2) Subtract one from a running total

        (3) Store a total (any number of totals can be stored)

c. Logic — the mechanical man can decide what instruction he will carry out next on the basis of answers to the following questions:

(1) Arithmetic results

(a) Is the result positive?

(b) Is the result negative?

(c) Is the result zero?

(d) Is the result equal to a predetermined amount?

(2) Physical status

(a) Are the raised arms touching anything?

B

Exploring the Visual Basic .NET IDE and Debugging

Appendix B explains how to use the Visual Basic .NET integrated development environment more effectively. The appendix covers topics including changing screen resolution, rearranging windows and toolbars in the Visual Basic .NET IDE, and using profiles to change the environment to meet your needs. The appendix also covers debugging techniques that you can use to fix syntax errors, logic errors, and run-time errors.

Changing Screen Resolution

Many programmers find it convenient to display as many of the windows and toolbars as possible while working in the Visual Basic .NET IDE. Professional software programmers typically work in as high a resolution as their computer will allow, in order to display many of these tools at all times. Some work with multiple monitors attached to the same computer in order to see as much information as possible.

When working on a project in Visual Basic .NET, you should set your computer monitor to as high a resolution as you can view comfortably, so that you can display multiple windows and toolbars. The screens shown in this book use a 1024 × 768 resolution. The following steps show how to change your screen's resolution to 1024 × 768 pixels, which is the screen resolution used in this book.

1. Click the Start button on the Windows taskbar and then click Control Panel on the Start menu.
2. Click the Appearance and Themes category and then click the Change the screen resolution task.
3. Drag the Screen resolution trackbar to the right or left until the screen resolution below the trackbar reads 1024 by 768 pixels as shown in Figure B-1.
4. Click the OK button and then click the Close button on the Appearance and Themes window title bar.

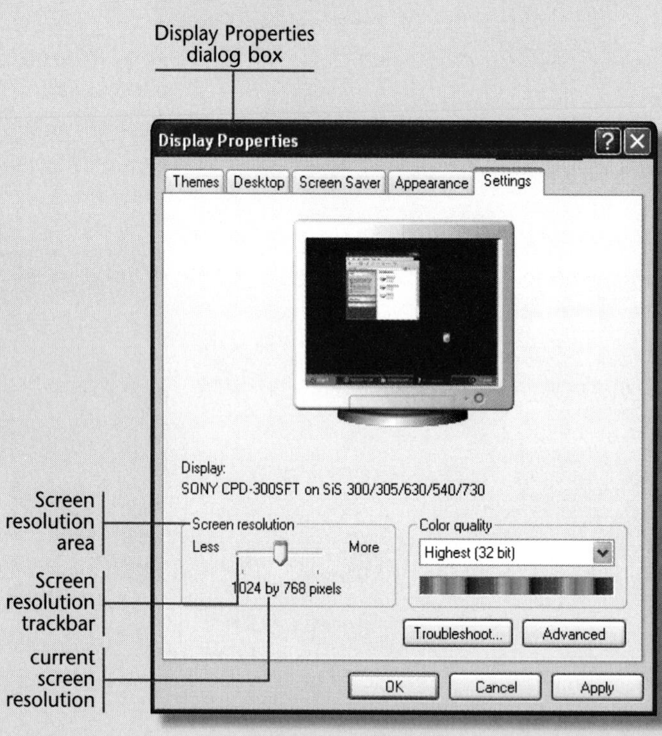

FIGURE B-1

You can experiment with various screen resolutions. Depending on your monitor and the video adapter installed in your computer, the screen resolutions available on your computer will vary.

When designing a user interface in the IDE, remember to take into consideration the screen resolutions available to the majority of the users of the application. A good rule of thumb is to test your application in all of the screen resolutions in which the application likely is to be used.

Customizing the Integrated Development Environment

The Visual Basic .NET integrated development environment (IDE) can be customized in a number of ways to help you work more efficiently. You quickly can change the look of the environment to your liking. The following sections show how to modify the IDE by selecting a profile and docking and undocking windows.

Selecting a Profile

As described, the Visual Basic .NET IDE contains the windows and toolbars that allow you to develop Visual Basic .NET applications and components. Visual Basic .NET records the size and location of these windows and toolbars when you close a project, so the IDE displays the same configuration each time you start Visual Basic .NET.

If you are a student working in a computer lab, the IDE may look completely different every time you start Visual Basic .NET on a computer in the lab, which can be disorienting if you are new to Visual Basic .NET. To help solve that problem, Visual Basic .NET includes several profiles that customize the environment in which you work. In Visual Basic .NET, a profile is used to store personalized settings that define the layout of windows, keyboard shortcuts, the default filter to use when searching for help, and other options in the Visual Basic .NET IDE. Once you choose a profile, Visual Basic .NET remembers it for the next time you use Visual Basic .NET on that computer.

As your proficiency in Visual Basic .NET improves, you can choose a different profile or modify the profile you already are using to change the settings for any existing projects and apply these settings when starting a new project. Each time you sit down at a computer in the lab, you should make sure to check the profile and modify it as described in this section.

The following steps show you how to customize the Visual Basic .NET environment by selecting a profile best suited for developing Visual Basic .NET programs.

1. After starting Visual Basic .NET, click the My Profile tab on the Start page.
2. Click the Profile box arrow and then click Visual Basic Developer in the Profile list (Figure B-2 on the next page).
3. Click the Projects tab on the Start page.

Figure B-2 shows the My Profile page after selecting the Visual Basic Developer profile. When the profile is selected, the Toolbox becomes docked to the left side of the IDE. The Keyboard Scheme, Window Layout, and Help Filter change to Visual Basic 6 and Visual Basic options. With the Help filter changed to Visual Basic, searches within Help only will display results for topics related to Visual Basic; topics related to other programming languages will be excluded.

Sample IDE Layouts

Figure B-3 on the next page shows a common layout for programmers developing Windows applications using Visual Basic .NET. The Task List is displayed at the bottom of the IDE. The Full Screen toolbar is docked to the right of the Standard toolbar. Clicking the Full Screen button on the Full Screen toolbar quickly changes the view of the main work area to a larger view. The larger view makes it easier to focus on that which you are working. The Debug toolbar is docked to the right of the Layout toolbar.

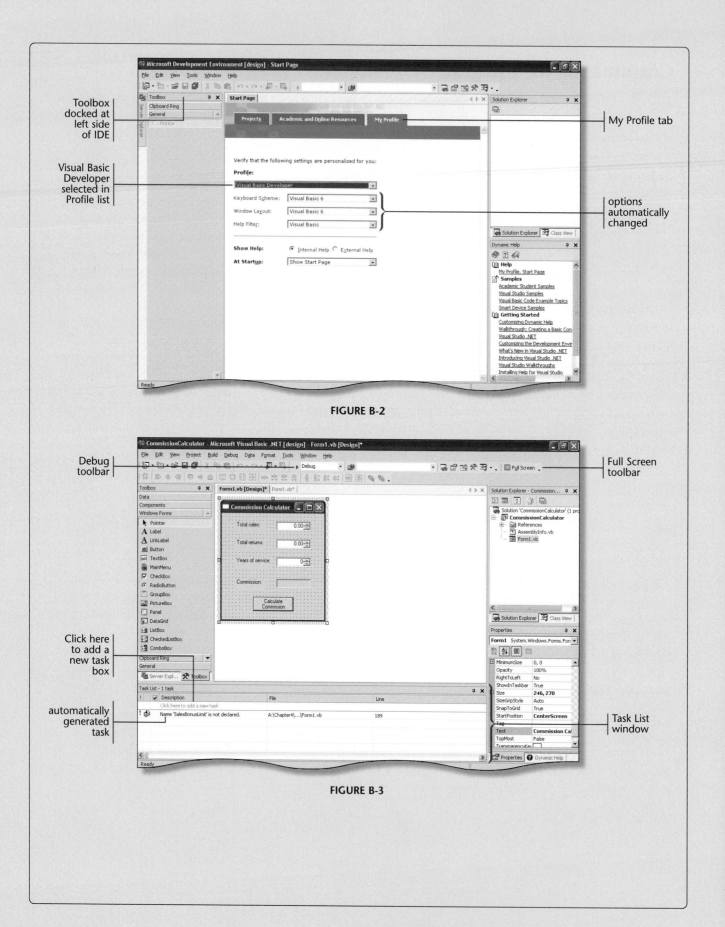

Toolbox docked at left side of IDE

Visual Basic Developer selected in Profile list

My Profile tab

options automatically changed

FIGURE B-2

Debug toolbar

Full Screen toolbar

Click here to add a new task box

automatically generated task

Task List window

FIGURE B-3

As you are working, Visual Basic .NET automatically generates a new task in the Task List for any syntax errors in your code (Figure B-3). The tasks in the Task List serve as reminders of things that must be completed before you are done working on the code. You also can add tasks or reminders to the Task List by clicking the Click here to add a new task box directly above the Task List.

Figure B-4 shows the result of undocking a window from the IDE. This technique is useful if your computer only supports lower screen resolutions. By undocking the windows, you can move some windows out of the way, but still have quick access to the windows when necessary. To undock a window, drag the title bar of the window until you see a floating outline of the window, and then release the mouse button. To dock an undocked window, drag the window to the upper, lower, left, or right edge of the IDE. An outline of the window will snap to the edge as you move the mouse pointer towards the edge where you want to dock the window. When the window snaps to the desired position, release the mouse button to dock the window.

Figure B-4 also shows the use of multiple tab groups. You can split the main work area into multiple tab groups by right-clicking a tab and then clicking the New Horizontal Tab Group command or the New Vertical Tab Group command.

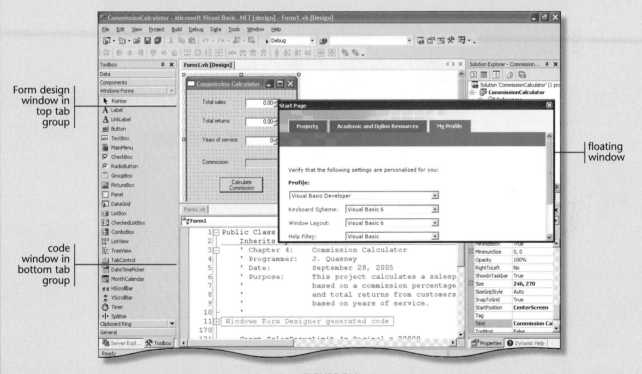

FIGURE B-4

Often, windows in the IDE may get cluttered or lost. To set the IDE back to its original state, click the Options command on the Tools menu and then click the Reset Window Layout button in the General page of the Environment options group.

Opening an Existing Project

You can open an existing project you have recently modified from the Project tab on the Start page. As shown in Figure B-5, the Projects tab on the Start page lists the name and last modified date for any projects on which you recently have worked. The following steps show you how to open the Commission Calculator project after it has been saved on the A: drive.

1. Start Visual Basic .NET and, if necessary, click the Projects tab on the Start page.
2. Click the Open Project button.
3. When the Open Project dialog box is displayed, use the Look in box to navigate to the location of the saved project. For the project shown in Figure B-5, the file location is the A:\Project1\CommissionCalculator folder.
4. Click the CommissionCalculator.sln file (Figure B-5).
5. Click the Open button.

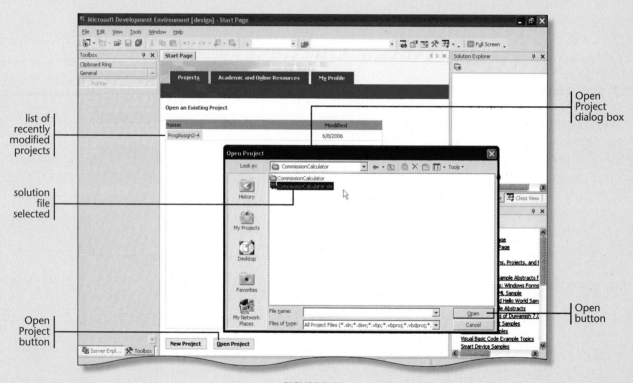

FIGURE B-5

The CommissionCalculator.sln file is the solution file that contains all of the information about the CommissionCalculator project. The next time you start Visual Basic .NET after opening the Commission Calculator project, you will see the Commission Calculator project listed. Instead of clicking the Open Project button to open the project, you can click the project name to open the project.

Debugging

Visual Basic .NET provides several methods you can use to find the portion of a program that includes an error. These methods are called **debugging techniques**. The errors themselves are called **bugs**, and the process of detecting the bugs is called **debugging**.

Three general categories of errors that require debugging include syntax errors, logic errors, and run-time errors. A **syntax error** occurs when you violate a rule of the Visual Basic .NET language. A **logic error** occurs when a program does not behave as intended, due to poor design or incorrect implementation of the design. A **run-time error**, often called an **exception**, is an error that occurs when conditions arise during run time that Visual Basic .NET does not know how to handle.

The following debugging process should be used to find and fix errors with the assistance of the Visual Basic .NET debugging tools:

- Determine the symptoms of an error
- Reproduce the error
- Determine which code statements are causing the error
- Fix the code statements
- Test the modified code to ensure that no unwanted side effects occur as a result of the modifications

Fixing Syntax Errors

When Visual Basic .NET detects a syntax error, it takes two actions. First, IntelliSense underlines the syntax error in the code window with a blue, wavy underline (Figure B-6). When you move the mouse pointer over the syntax error, IntelliSense displays a description of the syntax error. Second, an entry is added to the Task List window to remind you that you must fix the error. The entry includes a description of the error and a line number indicating where the error occurs in the code.

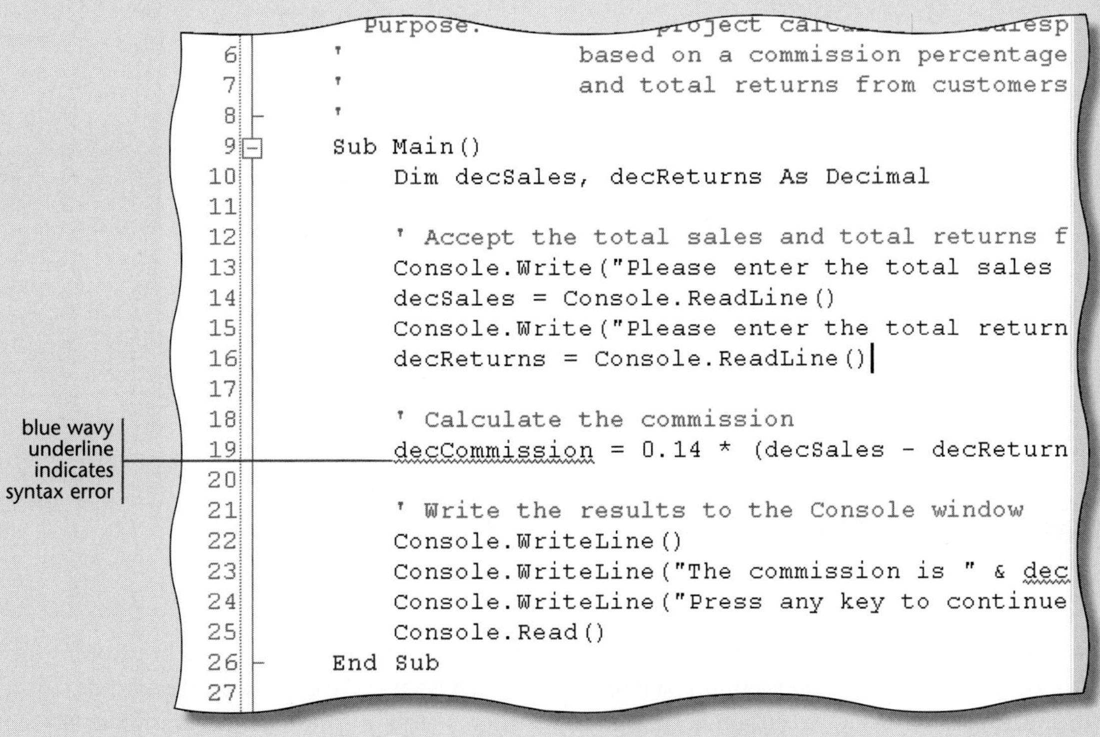

```
 6          '               based on a commission percentage
 7          '               and total returns from customers
 8       -  '
 9       -  Sub Main()
10              Dim decSales, decReturns As Decimal
11
12              ' Accept the total sales and total returns f
13              Console.Write("Please enter the total sales
14              decSales = Console.ReadLine()
15              Console.Write("Please enter the total return
16              decReturns = Console.ReadLine()|
17
18              ' Calculate the commission
19              decCommission = 0.14 * (decSales - decReturn
20
21              ' Write the results to the Console window
22              Console.WriteLine()
23              Console.WriteLine("The commission is " & dec
24              Console.WriteLine("Press any key to continue
25              Console.Read()
26       -  End Sub
27
```

blue wavy underline indicates syntax error

FIGURE B-6

If you attempt to run the project in the IDE while the code contains a syntax error, Visual Basic .NET displays a warning in a dialog box, indicating that errors exist in the code. The dialog box allows you to choose whether you want to continue execution despite the errors. If you choose to continue executing the code with syntax errors, the lines that contain the errors will not be accessible during run time. If the syntax error is severe enough, the entire procedure that contains the error may not be accessible during run time.

To fix a syntax error, navigate the code window to the line of code that contains the error. The Task List window includes a list of all syntax errors currently in the code. Move the mouse pointer over the underlined code to see a description of the error. Correct the error that is described in the pop-up window.

Setting Breakpoints

To help you find and fix logic errors, Visual Basic .NET includes tools that allow you to set a **breakpoint** in a program to pause the program (Figure B-7) and to watch and modify variables during run time. For example, you can set a breakpoint on a code statement during design time. The Breakpoints window contains a list of breakpoints currently set for code statements in the project. When the program is run in the IDE; the breakpoint causes the execution of code to pause at the statement. For example, as shown in Figure B-7 after a breakpoint is set in line 20, Visual Basic .NET halts execution of the Commission Calculator program at the breakpoint at line 20 during run time. After the program has paused at a breakpoint, you can instruct Visual Basic .NET to resume execution by clicking the Continue button or execute the code line by line — which is described in the next section.

Continue button causes execution to continue at line 20

Line 20 has control and is a breakpoint

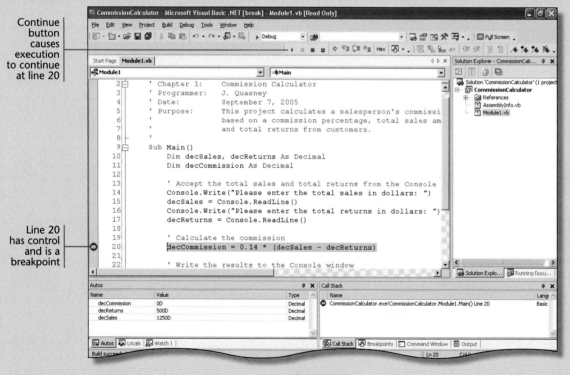

FIGURE B-7

Breakpoints help you find logic errors or run-time errors during design time. You can set a breakpoint for any line in the program where you want execution to pause, so you can review the code. The breakpoint tells Visual Basic .NET to pause (or break) execution at that point or when a certain condition occurs. To set a breakpoint, move the insertion point to the appropriate line and then use one of the following techniques:

- Click in the column to the left of the line number
- Right-click the line and then click the Insert Breakpoint command on the code window shortcut menu
- Select the line and then click New Breakpoint on the Debug menu
- Select the line and press the F9 key
- Select the line and press CTRL+B

When you set a breakpoint at design time, the code window displays the line highlighted in red and a filled red circle icon appears to the left of the line. When you execute the program after setting one or more breakpoints, Visual Basic .NET halts execution each time a breakpoint receives control, opens the code window, and highlights the line where the breakpoint paused execution in yellow, as shown in Figure B-7.

To remove a breakpoint, move the insertion point to the line where the breakpoint is set and then press the F9 key. You also can right-click the line where the breakpoint is set and then click the Remove Breakpoint command on the code window shortcut menu. An alternative method for clearing breakpoints is to select the Clear All Breakpoints command on the Debug menu or press CTRL+SHIFT+F9. This technique can be useful if you have a number of breakpoints set and want to clear all of them quickly.

Stepping and DataTips

When Visual Basic .NET encounters a breakpoint during run time, it enters break mode. When the program is in break mode, you can do one of the following:

1. Press the F8 key (Step Into command on the Debug menu) to enter step mode and execute one statement at a time
2. Display the values of variables
3. Delete or add new breakpoints
4. Click the Continue button (or press the F5 key) to continue execution of the program

As noted above, the Step Into command (F8 key) on the Debug menu is used to execute the program one statement at a time while the program is in **break mode**. When you click the Step Into command or press the F8 key, Visual Basic .NET enters step mode and then displays the first executable statement highlighted in yellow. Thereafter, each time you press the F8 key, Visual Basic .NET executes the highlighted statement and then displays the next executable statement with a yellow highlight. Using stepping with breakpoints allows you to pause execution at a certain point using a breakpoint and then continue execution using stepping, so you watch the logic of the code from the breakpoint forward.

When Visual Basic .NET is in break mode, you cannot modify code. You can, however, determine the current value of variables. **DataTips** provide the quickest method of viewing the values of variables that are not objects. To view the value of a variable using a DataTip, you place the insertion point over the variable anywhere in the code window during break mode. Figure B-8 on the next page shows the result of pressing the F8 key once after the program breaks at line 20. Placing the mouse pointer over a variable name during break mode displays a DataTip that shows the current value of the variable. For example, as shown in Figure B-8, the DataTip shows the value of the *decCommission* variable at that point in the execution of the code.

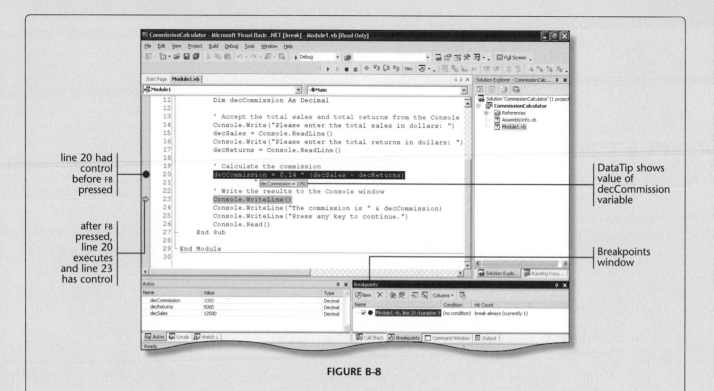

line 20 had control before F8 pressed

after F8 pressed, line 20 executes and line 23 has control

DataTip shows value of decCommission variable

Breakpoints window

FIGURE B-8

To modify code, you must exit break mode and return to design mode, modify the code, and then begin run time again to test your changes. To exit break mode, press the F5 key. Pressing the F5 key tells Visual Basic .NET to continue normal execution of the program, if no run-time errors have occurred. If you want to enter break mode again, press CTRL+BREAK. To return to normal execution of the program again, you can do one of the following:

1. Click the Continue button on the Debug toolbar (or press the F5 key) to continue normal execution.
2. Click Debug on the menu bar and then click the Step Into command (or press the F8 key) to activate step mode.

General Forms of Common Visual Basic .NET Statements, Data Types, and Naming Conventions

Appendix C summarizes the common Visual Basic .NET statements presented in this book along with their general forms. The naming conventions for variables and controls used in this book also are included.

General Forms of Visual Basic .NET Statements

Table C-1 summarizes the general forms of Visual Basic .NET statements introduced in this book and the page number on which the general forms appear.

Table C-1 General Forms of Common Visual Basic .NET Statements

STATEMENT	GENERAL FORM	PAGE NUMBER
Assignment	1. variable = newvalue 2. variable = result of expression	13
Comment	1. ' comment 2. REM comment 3. code 'comment	8
Constant Declaration	1. Const name As type = value 2. Const name = value	42
Dim (array)	1. Dim arrayname(upperlimit) As datatype 2. Dim arrayname() As datatype = { initialvalue1, initialvalue2...} 3. Dim arrayname() As datatype where arrayname represents the array name and upperlimit represents the upper-bound value of the array. The upperlimit parameter can be repeated and separated by commas to define multidimensional arrays. Similarly, commas can be placed in the parentheses in form 2 to define additional dimensions. For all one-dimensional arrays, the number of elements in the array is equal to upperlimit + 1, because the first element of all one-dimensional arrays has an index of 0. If initial values are given, the array must not be given an upperlimit in the declaration.	59
Dim (simple)	1. Dim variablename As datatype = initialvalue 2. Dim variablename As datatype 3. Dim variablename, variablename As datatype 4. Dim variablename	11

Do Until	1. Do Until condition
	    statements
	Loop
	2. Do
	    statements
	Loop Until condition
		63

Do While	1. Do While condition
	    statements
	Loop
	2. Do
	    statements
	Loop While condition
		63

Exit	1. Exit statement where statement is For or Do.	72

Table C-1 General Forms of Common Visual Basic .NET Statements (continued)

STATEMENT	GENERAL FORM	PAGE NUMBER

For...Next	1. For k = initial value To limit value Step increment value
	        statements within For...Next loop
	  Next k
	2. For k = initial value To limit value
	        statements within For...Next loop
	  Next k
	3. For k As Integer = initial value to limit value
	        statements within For...Next loop
	  Next k
	where k is a simple numeric variable called the loop variable, and the initial value, limit value, and increment value are numeric expressions.
		70

Function	1. Function name(argument 1, ..., argument n) As datatype
	        statements
	  End Function
	2. Private Function name(argument 1, ..., argument n) As datatype
	        statements
	  End Function
	where the Function name is a valid name following the conventions of variable naming.
		97

If...Then...Else	1. If condition Then clause 1 Else clause 2
	2. If condition Then clause 1 clause 2
	  Else
	      clause 3
	  End If
	3. If condition Then
	      clause
	  End If
	where condition is a relation that is either true or false and clause is a statement or series of statements. The Else keyword and subsequent clause are optional, as shown above in General form 3. General form 1 is called a single-line If...Then...Else statement; General forms 2 and 3 are called block If...Then...Else statements.
		34

Select Case	Select Case testexpression
	    Case matchexpression
	        [statements]
	
	        .
	        .
	        .
	
	    Case Else
	        [statements]
	End Select
	where testexpression is a string or numeric variable or expression that is matched with the matchexpression in the corresponding Case clauses; and matchexpression is a numeric or string expression or a range of numeric or string expressions of the following form:
	1. expression, expression, . . . , expression
	2. expression To expression
	3. a relational expression where relation is <, >, >=, <=, =, or <>
		47

Visual Basic .NET Data Types and Naming Convention

Table C-2 summarizes the Visual Basic .NET data types and the recommended naming convention for the three-character prefix preceding variable names of the corresponding data type.

Table C-2 Visual Basic .NET Data Types and Naming Convention

CATEGORY	DATA TYPE	DESCRIPTION	RANGE	PREFIX
Character	Char	16-bit (2 bytes) character	1 16-bit character	chr
	String	Sequence of 0 or more 16-bit characters	0 to 2,147,483,647 16-bit characters	str
Integral	Short	16-bit (2 bytes) integer value	-32,768 to 32,767	shr
	Integer	32-bit (4 bytes) integer value	-2,147,483,648 to 2,147,483,647	int
	Long	64-bit (8 bytes) integer value	-9,223,372,036,854,775,808 to 9,223,372,036,854,775,807	lng
	Byte	8-bit (1 byte) unsigned integer value	0 to 255	byt
Nonintegral	Decimal	128-bit (16 bytes) fixed point	1.0e-28 to 7.9e28	dec
	Single	32-bit floating point	±1.5e-45 to ±3.4e38	sng
	Double	64-bit floating point	±5.0e-324 to ±1.7e308	dbl
Miscellaneous	Boolean	32-bit value	True or False	bln
	Date	64-bit signed integer — each increment represents 100 nanoseconds elapsed since the beginning of January 1 in the year 1	January 1, 0001:00:00:00 to December 31, 9999:23:59:59	dtm
	Object	32-bit number that represents the location of the object in memory	Any object	obj

Visual Basic .NET Control Naming Convention

Table C-3 summarizes the naming convention used in this book for naming controls. Use the three letters in the second column as a prefix to a meaningful name.

Table C-3 Control Naming Convention

CONTROL	PREFIX
Button	btn
Label	lbl
NumericUpDown	nud
TextBox	txt

D

Programming Fundamentals Best Practices

Appendix D lists the Best Practices tips presented throughout this book, in order by chapter. The first column contains the page number on which the corresponding Best Practice in the second column is presented. Use the page number to review the topics to which the Best Practice applies in greater detail. Use the second column as a quick overview of the Best Practices.

Chapter 1 Best Practices

PAGE NUMBER	BEST PRACTICE
4	Use flowcharts or pseudocode to solidify the design of every program you develop. Continue to use and update the flowcharts or pseudocode as you enhance or modify the program.
8	Use comments to remind yourself and other programmers of the purpose of code. Use comments in the following two ways: 1. Place a comment that identifies the module and its purpose at the top of every file that contains code. This type of comment typically is called a comment header. 2. Place comments near portions of code that need clarification or serve an important purpose.
9	Comments should be entered along the way, as you enter program code, rather than at the end. Writing comments as you work helps you clarify the purpose of code for your own reference. After the program is complete, the comments can help you create the program documentation outside of the code.
10	When selecting the data type to use for a variable or constant, try to use the data type that takes up the smallest amount of memory. Use an integral data type if a variable or constant will not contain a decimal amount; use a nonintegral data type if a variable or constant might contain a decimal; and use a Decimal data type if a variable or constant will contain a currency value.
12	When naming variables, use names that describe the purpose of the variable, such as decSales to store a decimal value for sales numbers or intAvailSeats to store an integer value for the number of seats available on a flight. Using descriptive names helps clarify the purpose of the variable and makes the code easier to understand.
16	When coding a numeric expression, use parentheses freely when in doubt as to the valid form and evaluation of a numeric expression. Adding parentheses helps to provide clarity when you are writing code or a program is evaluating an expression.
18	You should save your work periodically while you are working on a project and again before you run the project. Make backups of your work that you can store in a separate physical location.

Chapter 2 Best Practices

PAGE NUMBER	BEST PRACTICE
35	For readability purposes, avoid the single-line If…Then…Else statement. Instead, use a block If…Then…Else statement and always code the statement with the End If keyword.
37	Negating a relation usually is preferred when a program must execute additional tasks as a result of the condition being false.
38	Avoid excessive nesting of If…Then…Else structures when possible, in order to improve readability of your code.
39	Because the Not logical operator can increase the complexity of a decision statement significantly, use it sparingly.
43	A constant or variable always should be declared with a data type. Code is more efficient and foolproof if all constants and variables are defined explicitly with a data type.
46	Use the Select Case statement when more than two alternatives exist in an If…Then…Else structure.

Chapter 3 Best Practices

PAGE NUMBER	BEST PRACTICE
60	Use line-continuation characters to break long lines of code over several lines in the code window, in order to make your code more readable. When entering a line-continuation character, enter a space, enter the line-continuation character (_), and then press the ENTER key. The space is required before the line-continuation character (_) and no spaces are allowed after the line-continuation character (_).
64	If the decision to terminate is at the top of the loop, use Do While or Do Until. If the decision to terminate is at the bottom of the loop, use Do Loop While or Do Loop Until. Use the While keyword if you want to continue execution of the loop while the condition is true. Use the Until keyword if you want to continue execution of the loop until the condition is true.
64	When implementing a Do While structure, always use the statement that does not require a negated relational operator, because it is easier to read.
66	Use the concatenation operators whenever possible in assignment statements to make code more readable.
69	When possible, use a For...Next statement as opposed to a Do While statement because it is easier to read, uses less memory, is more efficient, and executes faster.
72	Use the Exit statement sparingly in order to keep the logic of code more readable. Typically, the use of the Exit statement is reserved for use when an error condition or unusual circumstance occurs within a loop.

Chapter 4 Best Practices

PAGE NUMBER	BEST PRACTICE
82	When working on form design, display the Toolbox. When you need more room in the IDE for such tasks as coding, use the Auto Hide button on the Toolbox to hide the Toolbox.
85	When building a user interface in Visual Basic .NET, you should use the following three-step method: 1) create the interface 2) set properties of controls 3) write code
86	Take some time to learn more about Visual Basic .NET controls by experimenting with the various controls and reading information about controls in Visual Basic .NET Help. While many controls are very flexible, always be careful to choose the right control for the job. For example, if you want a user to select one item from a list, use a ListBox control or a group of RadioButton controls, rather than having the user type the selection in a TextBox control.
87	When working with forms, you may find it is faster to add all of the required controls to the form and then position them correctly on the form.
88	Use Label controls to display text on a form that will not be modified at run time.
88	Use NumericUpDown controls for numeric input where you want to limit the range of allowed input values to fall between a minimum and maximum value.
89	Use TextBox controls for input and output values on a form that may change during run time.
91	Use a standard naming convention when naming controls. For example, use three-letter prefixes for control names, such as txt for TextBox controls, lbl for Label controls, nud for NumericUpDown controls, and btn for Button controls.
93	Take the time to fine-tune your user interface by setting such properties as the TabIndex and TabStop properties. Such detail is noticed by users and makes your program operate in a manner familiar to users of Windows applications.

continued on the next page

Chapter 4 Best Practices (continued)

PAGE NUMBER	BEST PRACTICE
94	Use the AcceptButton form property to designate a default button on a form. Use the CancelButton form property to designate a cancel or reset button on the form.
97	Use function procedures in your code when your design calls for a specific calculation or operations that may be used several times in your code and whose end result is a single value.

Index